THE WELL-DRESSED SALAD

FRESH, DELICIOUS AND SATISFYING RECIPES

JENNIFER JOYCE

PAVILION

Contents

Introduction

My obsession with salads began in childhood. I grew up in rural Wisconsin in America, surrounded by lush orchards and fertile farmland. My father, Leo, kept an enormous vegetable garden to help feed our family of 11. Although I cursed the long hours of weeding and laborious end-of-summer bottling, I loved the earthy smell of the garden, its astounding variety and eating juicy, ripe vegetables straight off the vine. My Italian mother, Louise, had to be an efficient household manager, of course, but she was also an artful cook. Delicious food was the one extravagance allowed. Since vegetables were plentiful, we had salads with every meal. Most were simple but intensely good: cucumbers, onions and tomatoes or roasted (bell) peppers dressed with red wine vinegar and olive oil. My favourite part of eating salad came at its pungent end. I would wipe the last vinegary remnants with bread and savour the final tart tastes. It's those mouth-watering memories that spur me to seek out ingredients as exceptional as the produce grown in my father's garden and transformed at my mother's table.

In the 20 years I've lived in London, England, my cooking has been influenced by many different cultures and synthesized into what I call modern ethnic food. Although the classes I teach each week might cover Vietnamese or Middle Eastern cooking, Californian cuisine or North African tastes, all my dishes have one thing in common – the pursuit of bold, fresh flavours. I am passionate about combining herbs, vinegars and unusual ethnic products to create extraordinary flavours. You won't, for instance, find many mayonnaise dressings here, because flavours should be enhanced, not smothered. I decided to write this book after designing a class on salads and found it difficult to pare down my choices. I love them all, from the great Thai varieties to the perfect Greek salad. I also began to realize how well salads slot into our current lifestyle, reflecting our new awareness about healthy eating. They are wholesome, light and yet full of flavour. A salad is no longer simply a side dish – an uninspired bowl of iceberg lettuce slathered with bottled dressing. It's the star of the meal.

My childhood hours in a garden piqued my interest in vibrant salads. But to know the pleasures of good food, you don't need to grow it, you need spectacular new ways to prepare it. Open this book to any page, assemble a few ingredients and eat well!

Salad leaves

Salad leaves (greens) are the backbone for most salads, adding texture, taste and glorious colour. An extra bonus is that they contain an abundance of nutrients and contain few calories. The general rule is the darker the colour, the more nutrients the leaves contain. Most are rich in vitamins A and C, but some such as spinach contain iron. Growing your own salad leaves couldn't be easier, but if green fingers evade you, there is a huge selection available to buy. These days, supermarkets are introducing new lettuces and baby leaves and our excitement can rapidly turn to confusion owing to the myriad varieties. Don't feel overwhelmed – use the groupings in this guide to identify the different types.

MILD LEAVES

These sweet and subtle leaves feature in the ubiquitous tossed green salad, but they work equally well in more sophisticated creations. Strong flavours were made for these leaves. Piquant cheeses such as feta, Parmesan and Gorgonzola pair well, along with garlicky vinaigrettes and creamy dressings. Delicate round lettuce (butterhead) is ideal for South-east Asian salads with their bracing chilli-lime dressings. Spinach and cos (romaine) lettuce are the workhorses of this group. Their crisp texture keeps well once they've been dressed.

Red oak leaf lettuce
Lollo rosso
Lollo bionda
Round (butterhead)
Boston
Iceberg (crisphead)

Lamb's lettuce (mâche)
Spinach
Cos (romaine) lettuce
Little Gem (Bibb) lettuce

SPICY-PEPPERY LEAVES

Velvety soft in texture but spicy in taste, peppery leaves are perfect for flavourful olive oils and vinegars, citrus vinaigrettes and Asian soy and garlicky dressings. Combine a couple of varieties, rather than using just one alone. They also work well mixed with mild lettuces or bitter leaves, such as chicory (Belgian endive). Most often, you will find the baby leaves sold together as mesclun. This mixture is usually made up of baby chard, baby mustard leaves, rocket (arugula) and mizuna. Sophisticated and full of taste, mesclun can make an excellent salad on its own with a simple vinaigrette. For added glamour, try adding edible flowers, such as nasturtiums.

Watercress
Rocket (arugula)
Mizuna
Baby kale
Tatsoi
Baby mustard leaves
Baby beetroot tops (beet greens)
Baby chard

BITTER LEAVES

Prized for their lovely texture and unique bitter taste, these hearty leaves cry out for counterparts such as toasted nuts, fried pancetta and blue cheese. They are magnificent when dressed with raspberry, sherry and balsamic vinegars, nut oils, and warm vinaigrettes with garlic and anchovies. Frisée (curly endive) is essential for French salads with warm goat's cheese, poached eggs or crispy bacon. Radicchio is crucial to the Italians' insalata mista and its vivid red brightens any dull colours. Don't just stop at serving these leaves raw, they are also superb when grilled (broiled) or braised.

Radicchio
Treviso (red chicory)
Chicory (Belgian endive)
Frisée (curly endive)
Escarole
Dandelion leaves

CABBAGES

These ubiquitous vegetables have sadly endured a downtrodden reputation. They make the most colourful, crunchy and delicious salads that can sit in the dressing for days without relinquishing their texture. Coleslaws and warm winter salads are where they are used most. Crisp, raw chopped vegetables, such as onions, (bell) peppers and carrots make lovely additions. Dressings can range from tangy mayonnaise-based to tart vinaigrettes with celery or caraway seeds. Chinese leaves (cabbage) is best for Asian coleslaws with a dressing made of rice wine vinegar and sesame seed oil.

Savoy
White
Green
Red
Chinese leaves (Napa cabbage/Chinese cabbage)

Pod power

Packed with vitamins, minerals and fibre, beans and lentils, also known as legumes, are astonishingly good for you. They also provide a wonderful foundation for a salad, soaking up the flavour of the dressing. Legumes are seeds contained within a pod and include peas, lentils and beans. Lentils, sometimes referred to as dhal, do not require pre-soaking (unlike beans) or take long to cook. When buying dried legumes, look for ones that are shiny and uniform in size and colour. Store for up to 6 months in a cool, dark place.

Although canned legumes are quick and convenient, cooked dried beans, peas and lentils retain their texture and have a better flavour. To prepare, put the dried beans in a bowl, cover with plenty of water and soak overnight, then drain. Transfer the beans to a pan, cover with plenty of fresh water and bring to the boil. Turn the heat down and simmer for 30 minutes or up to 2 hours until soft. Don't add salt until the last 10 minutes of cooking as it toughens the beans.

BEANS

Cannellini – Large oval beans with a creamy, mild flavour. Use in Mediterranean salads with tomatoes, fresh herbs and balsamic vinaigrettes.

Borlotti (cranberry/tongue of fire) – Plump, beige/burgundy-striped beans with a smooth texture and mild taste. Loves garlic, pancetta, tomatoes or any other Italian-style ingredients.

Haricot (great northern/navy) – These are small to medium white beans. They could be swapped for cannellini in salads, but their mild flavour is better suited to stews.

Flageolets – Creamy oval beans that are actually immature kidney beans. Their lovely moss-green colour is retained after boiling and they're excellent with olive oil and fresh herbs.

Broad (fava) – Predominantly eaten fresh instead of dried in salads. The tough, outer skins are best removed after cooking. Sharp cheeses suit them well.

Chickpeas (garbanzo beans) – Loved for their nutty flavour and creamy texture, these round beans are very versatile and go well with herbs, spices, yogurt, cheeses or spiky vinaigrettes.

Black-eyed beans (peas) – Round and white with a purple spot, they make interesting salads. Their sweet taste and starchy texture suit crispy bacon, greens and a cider or sherry vinegar dressing.

Aduki (adzuki) – Imported from Japan, these are small maroon beans with a white stripe. Nutty and sweet with a creamy texture, they partner well with crunchy vegetables, tofu (beancurd) and Asian or citrus dressings.

Black – Sometimes referred to as turtle beans, these little purple/black legumes have a delicious earthiness. They work well with fresh coriander (cilantro), tomatoes, mango and cumin.

Mung beans – Tiny green legumes with yellow centres, these can be ground to make cellophane noodles, or split into dhal (moong dhal) and are delicious with sharp dressings and salty cheeses.

Red kidney – These big red beans have a rich and meaty texture. Cumin, cider vinegar, chillies and other strong Latin American ingredients suit them.

Pinto/rattlesnake/appaloosa – These are all from the red kidney bean family, but are slightly smaller and oval-shaped. They share a creamy texture, strong beany flavour and lovely pale-brown colouring. Use in salads with smoky chipotle chillies, feta, lots of fresh coriander (cilantro).

LENTILS

Red – Very small and delicate lentils with an orange-red hue. They work well with cumin, roasted vegetables, feta or goat's cheese, fresh herbs and citrus dressings.

Yellow – Also referred to as pigeon or gunga peas, they have a wonderful yellow colour and soft texture. Combine with Indian flavours, such as yogurt, cumin and lemon.

Green and brown – The largest of the lentils, they both have a good flavour. They do not hold their shape well after cooking and become slightly mushy. For this reason, I prefer to use Puy in salads when available.

Puy – Small green and silver-flecked lentils sourced from the French region of Le Puy. Valued for their firm texture, they are unquestionably the best lentils for salads. They require shorter cooking times and work well with curry and spices.

Tomato intelligence

There are very few countries, with the exception of those in Asia, that do not embrace tomatoes. Originally from Peru, they were brought to the rest of the world by the Spanish conquistadors. Technically, they are fruits but are used in salads and cooking as a vegetable. Their intense colour is from lycopene, which is also a powerful antioxidant. They also contain high levels of vitamins A, C and E, which can be diminished during cooking, so eating tomatoes raw in salads provides the highest concentration of these vitamins.

Most tomatoes are sold under-ripe, so are best given a couple of days to finish maturing. Their favourite home is a wire or wicker basket that allows air to circulate. Refrigeration changes the texture of the flesh and prevents them from ripening further.

There are hundreds of names for different tomato varieties, which can change depending on region or country. Stay clear of names such as Moneymaker, Red Ponderosa or Mortgage Lifter; although commercially successful, these varieties are not renowned for their flavour. When choosing tomatoes for salads, think about what kind of taste, texture and colour you are looking for. Each type is based on shape and size, with texture, flavour, and water and seed content varying depending on variety.

BEEFSTEAK

The largest of all the tomatoes, beefsteak, beef or heirloom have a dense texture, few seeds and an excellent flavour, which is ideal for sliced tomato salads. They must be left to ripen before using or they'll have little taste; the unripened green specimens will eventually turn red if they are left for long enough. The beefsteak's sturdy texture means that it is also particularly good coated in polenta (cornmeal) and pan-fried. The best variety to look for is the Marmande, which has a bumpy and irregular shape and is sourced from Provence or Sicily. Delice (French) or Momotaro (British) are also good choices with juicy flesh and a sweet taste.

PLUM

Oval- or pear-shaped, these tomatoes range from small to medium. They are sometimes called Roma, as they are predominately grown and exported from southern Italy. The San Marzano variety is particularly elongated in shape and mostly used for high-quality canned tomatoes. Prized for their meaty flesh, sweet taste and low water content, they are perfect for chopping or roasting. Both yellow and red varieties are grown, but the latter is more dependable for flavour. The small egg-shaped plum tomatoes are called pomodorino (Italian or Spanish), Santa (British), Midi (British) or Grape (American). Gorgeously sweet and available most of the year, these are invaluable in winter when the tomato selection is poor.

CHERRY

These have the highest sugar content of all tomatoes, which explains why they taste so sweet. Despite their tough skins, they are juicy and delicious and work best left whole or simply halved. Red is the predominant colour, but they are also grown in yellow, gold and orange varieties, with names such as Sungold or Golden Delight. They are sold either by weight or packaged as vine-ripened, still attached to the stem. In both cases, the quality can vary so use your discretion. Not seen very often, the red and yellow teardrop tomatoes are particularly good for colour and taste. They are more likely to be found at farmers' markets than grocery stores.

ROUND

The ubiquitous standard tomato seen in most stores is medium in size, full-fleshed, but heavy with seeds and water. They are best for slicing or cutting into quarters. Most are sold commercially and extremely under-ripe, so it's best to give them 2 days minimum to gain some colour. Soil-grown, organic or vine-ripened are the most notable and tasty. The yellow variety, called Sunburst, has a bright yellow or golden colour, but sadly not much flavour. Some popular red British varieties are the Regency, Rochelle (vine-ripened) or Gardener's Delight. Hydroponic or hothouse tomatoes are tasteless creations that should be avoided at all times unless desperate.

Asian noodle know-how

Supreme in Asian culture and cuisine, noodles are eaten enthusiastically for breakfast, lunch and dinner. Heads bowed over bowls of noodles is a familiar sight all over Asia. Fat, skinny, round or flat, noodles make interesting salads tossed with soy or lime dressings. The numerous types and shapes of noodles can be overwhelming, so use this guide to make sure that you are getting the right one. Let your intuition guide you on added ingredients. Seared duck breast, seafood, chillies, spring onions (scallions) and julienned vegetables are just a few, but let your creativity flow.

WHEAT NOODLES

Made from a flour and water base, these sometimes also include egg. All of these varieties need to be boiled before using. Most can be purchased in the Asian section of a supermarket or Asian food stores.

Chinese egg noodles – Bright yellow noodles that can be thick or thin and available in fresh or dried form. Hearty additions, such as spicy peanut sauce, seared duck or shredded pork, work well with them.

Chinese wheat noodles – Mainly sold dried in individual "nest" portions at Chinese food stores and supermarkets. The size varies from thick to thin and they are made round or flat. Toss with an Asian pesto or vibrant dressings.

Ramen noodles – Made from wheat flour, salt, water and kansui (an alkaline solution), these Japanese noodles fare better in soups than salads as their delicate texture is not sturdy

enough for most dressings. They are sold fresh or dried, thick, thin or ribbon-like in Japanese food stores and some supermarkets.

Somen noodles – Elegant in their ribbon-tied bundles, these delicate thin, white noodles are from Japan. Best served simply with a soy dressing, or tossed with chilli, ginger and coriander (cilantro).

Udon noodles – Thick, white Japanese noodles sold fresh in vacuum packs or dried. Round, square or flat, udon are best suited to soy and ginger dressings, chillies and spring onions (scallions). They make a good side salad for grilled (broiled) Asian pork or braised pork belly (side).

RICE NOODLES

Produced from rice starch or rice flour, these noodles should be soaked in just-boiled water until soft. The soaking time varies depending on their thickness. Although they are more common in supermarkets, you may need to visit Asian food stores to find them.

Rice sticks – They range from very thin (similar to vermicelli), medium (fettuccine size), all the way up to large, flat Thai noodles called jantaboon. The thin and medium noodles are best for salads and work especially well with Thai, Chinese and Vietnamese flavours.

Thin rice vermicelli noodles – Tiny thread noodles used in Chinese, Thai and Vietnamese cooking. Sold in tidy bundles or thick, crinkled rafts, they are among the best noodles for salads.

Their bland nature is perfect for soaking up big flavours such as garlic, chilli and ginger. Not only used soft, they are also excellent deep-fried.

BEAN THREAD NOODLES

Visit a Thai or Chinese store to find these noodles made from mung bean starch, which simply need soaking in hot water before using.

Glass noodles – Also called cellophane noodles, they are valued for their transparent appearance after soaking and are particularly good with a lime juice and Thai fish sauce dressing as well as punchy herbs, including mint, coriander (cilantro) or Thai basil. They make delicious vegetarian salads and can also be mixed with paper-thin slices of seared beef, crab or juicy prawns (shrimp).

BUCKWHEAT (SOBA) NOODLES

Soba noodles – These pale-brown, protein-rich noodles are made from buckwheat and can be found in supermarkets and Japanese food stores. Cook them in boiling water for 1–2 minutes before using. Their sturdy texture and nutty taste produce outstanding salads and they can served chilled on ice with a dashi dipping sauce/ dressing or tossed with soy, garlic and crisp vegetables, such as broccoli.

Green tea noodles – Also called cha soba noodles, these Japanese noodles are soba noodles with green tea flavouring. Their pale, moss-green colour and green tea flavour mean they make interesting salads. Seared beef, teriyaki, asparagus, duck and spring onions (scallions) all complement them well.

Oils and vinegars

Creating a memorable salad is not difficult if you're armed with the right oils and vinegars. Even humble lettuce becomes aristocratic when adorned with a few drops of walnut oil and top-quality sherry vinegar. Avoid bland oils and cheap, throat-catching vinegars as they can sabotage salads made with good-quality ingredients and hard work. Instead, focus on brands with proper ageing, sharp flavours and good colour. Whether you use the classics or venture into the new genre of exciting oils and vinegars, focus on taste and quality.

VINEGARS

Balsamic – made from the white Trebbiano grape, this aged wine vinegar is intensely dark, powerfully aromatic and tastes both sweet and tart. It is sold in various grades and top of the table is Aceto Balsamico Tradizionale, which is aged in casks for a minimum of 12 years, making it expensive, exquisite and perfect for salad making – although it is best used for drizzling, rather than in large quantities for dressings. Factory-made brands aren't given the same loving care as the traditionally made, so they lack a real depth of flavour, but are still tasty. Italian or Mediterranean salads suit balsamic vinegar best.

White balsamic – Made by an entirely different process to dark balsamic vinegar, it is produced by combining Champagne vinegar with concentrated grape juice for a sweet white wine vinegar. It is lovely in mild dressings.

Cider vinegar – This hearty, golden-coloured vinegar is made from apples. Its fruity and tart nature works well in mayonnaise dressings, potato salads and coleslaws.

Champagne vinegar – A wine vinegar made from Champagne stock, before the bubbles in the second fermentation. With a delicate character and a clean taste, it is well suited to light vinaigrettes for vegetables and lettuces.

Rice vinegar – Both Japanese and Chinese vinegars are made from fermented white rice. It is delicate, with a pale, clear colour and a mild sweet and sour flavour. Brown rice vinegar is another variation. Pale amber in colour, it has slightly more depth than the white. Rice vinegar is best used in Asian slaws, noodles and aubergine (eggplant) salads.

Sherry vinegar – A Spanish vinegar, made from sweet Oloroso sherry, is aged for at least 10 years in oak casks until it is transformed into a complex, full-bodied vinegar. Raisin-like, smoky and nutty, it has an intense flavour that is particularly complementary to North African, Mexican and Spanish cuisines. Look for quality brands with the ageing listed on the label.

Wine vinegar – Made from red or white wine, this is the most popular vinegar. Depending on the maker, the colour, acidity and flavour can vary dramatically. White should be used in a similar way to Champagne vinegar. Particularly notable is the Chardonnay white, which has a sweet, subtle taste. The best red wine vinegars are made using the Orléans process in which high-quality wine is fermented in barrels for months. Italian, French and Spanish producers export the best quality. Look for the ruby-coloured Cabernet Sauvignon or Chianti varieties, which are intensely flavoured and low in acidity.

Flavoured vinegars – Made by infusing herbs or chillies into white wine vinegar, they have a clean, acidic flavour and herbaceous taste. Most are sold for decorative rather than culinary purposes. Tarragon vinegar is an exception, lending a tangy taste to pasta or rice salads. Quality can vary, so look carefully at the producer to avoid over-acidic brands. French imports are very good.

Fruit vinegars – The method for producing these varies from macerating fruit in white wine or Champagne vinegar to mixing purées into the vinegar. France is reputed for its raspberry vinegar, but there are many others available such as pear, blueberry, pineapple and mango. Cassis balsamic vinegar is slightly different, combining red wine vinegar with blackcurrant concentrate. Fruit vinegars are best used with nut oils for delicate mesclun (mixed young salad leaves) or salads involving fruit.

Black vinegar – A black-coloured vinegar made in China. It has a smoky, sweet flavour and is made from black rice or millet. It can be difficult to find, unless you shop in Asian food stores, so substitute with a light, inexpensive balsamic vinegar. Its unique taste complements noodles and soy-based dressings.

OILS

Olive oil – There are many different types and grades to choose from, some of which are still made using ancient techniques dating back to 3,000 bc. Historically, extra virgin olive oil was the first pressing of olives and then the lower graded olive oil the subsequent extraction, but with current manufacturing this isn't necessarily the case as many olive oils are now blends or chemically refined. Extra virgin remains the best for dressings but if I'm making mayonnaise, I tend to go for a lighter oil.

Extra virgin has a greeny-gold colour and a fruity to peppery flavour, which varies depending on its country of origin and producer. It is personal taste as to which country's oil you like best, but I rate Tuscan as the finest, with other Italian regions close behind. Spanish and Greek are slightly rougher with a hint of bitterness. French and Californian are mild, lacking the piquancy of the others. Extra virgin olive oil is my standard for making vinaigrette (other than for Asian dressings) as it complements almost everything.

Vegetable oils – Oils extracted from a single plant-type are labelled 'pure'; others called 'vegetable oil' are a mixture of different types. Most are low in cholesterol and comprise monounsaturated or polyunsaturated fats. There are numerous types: corn, grapeseed, rapeseed (canola), sunflower, soya and safflower oils being among the many. All share a mild, neutral taste that is useful for mayonnaise and other thick dressings.

Walnut and hazelnut oils – Aromatic and elegant, these oils are cold-pressed, which preserves their nutty taste. Unfortunately, they lose their fragrance and flavour fairly quickly so need to be used within 3 months of opening and it is best to store them in a cool, dark place. They are magnificent mixed with fruit or sherry vinegars for frisée (curly endive) or mesclun salads.

Groundnut (peanut oil) – Most groundnut oil is not cold-pressed and therefore has little or no flavour, although you can find cold-pressed with a true nutty taste in some Asian food stores. Groundnut is more expensive than vegetable oil and is respected for its high smoke point and lack of odour while frying. The Asian variety is particularly good in soy-based dressings.

Sesame oil – Olive and sesame are the oldest oils in history, dating back to the ancient Egyptians. Extracted from toasted sesame seeds, this dark oil has a nutty aroma and flavour, with most Asians using it for flavour accent. It is excellent in soy-based dressings for noodles, aubergines or poultry.

Pumpkin oil – A thick, robust oil made from roasted pumpkin seeds, it is dark green in colour. Strongly flavoured, pumpkin oil is best drizzled over grilled (broiled) vegetables or mixed with other oils for dressings.

Roasted red peppers with honey and pine nuts

Serve these simple peppers as part of an antipasti spread or use them to make simple crostini. The sweetness of the peppers melds beautifully with the honey and balsamic vinegar dressing, and roasting your own is easy and really worth the effort. Serve with bread or toasted crostini spread with ricotta (page 21).

**SERVES 4/PREP 15 MINUTES/
COOK 10 MINUTES**

7 red and/or yellow (bell) peppers, de-seeded
  and quartered
60g/2¼oz/½ cup pine nuts
3 tbsp chopped flat-leaf parsley leaves

HONEY DRESSING
3 tbsp extra virgin olive oil
2 large garlic cloves, thinly sliced
2 tbsp balsamic vinegar
2 tbsp clear honey
1 tsp salt
½ tsp freshly ground black pepper

Preheat the grill (broiler) to high. Place the peppers, skin-side up, on a large baking (cookie) sheet and grill (broil) until blackened. Place the peppers in a plastic bag, seal and set aside for 5 minutes.

Meanwhile, make the honey dressing. Heat the olive oil in a sauté pan and cook the garlic until golden, about 1 minute. Add the vinegar, honey, salt and pepper.

When the peppers are cool enough to handle, remove the skins but do not rinse. Thickly slice the flesh and place in a medium bowl. Pour the dressing over the roasted peppers and mix well until combined.

Sprinkle the pine nuts and parsley over the salad and toss again before serving.

GET ORGANIZED
The salad can be fully prepared and will keep for up to 2 days in the refrigerator. It's best served at room temperature.

Egyptian feta salad with dill and mint

Claudia Roden's time-honoured recipes burst with magical taste, and this salad was inspired by her book *The New Book of Middle Eastern Food*. Scoop up this fresh-tasting salad with crisp pitta triangles.

SERVES 4 AS A SNACK/PREP 10 MINUTES/
COOK 10 MINUTES

200g/7oz feta cheese, drained
3 tbsp extra virgin olive oil
juice of ½ lemon
2 small Lebanese cucumbers, trimmed and diced,
  or 1 medium cucumber, de-seeded and diced
1 small red onion, finely diced
2 tbsp chopped mint leaves
2 tbsp chopped flat-leaf parsley leaves
2 tbsp chopped dill

PITTA CRISPS
6 pitta breads
3 tbsp extra virgin olive oil
1 tsp paprika
salt and freshly ground black pepper

Preheat the oven to 200°C/400°F/Gas Mark 6. To make the pitta crisps, use a pair of scissors to cut around the outside of each pitta. Split them open and cut into triangles. Brush with the olive oil and season well with paprika, salt and pepper. Bake for 8–9 minutes or until golden, then leave to cool.

Crumble the feta into a bowl and mash with the olive oil and lemon juice. Season with black pepper. Add the cucumber, onion and chopped herbs and mix gently. Taste and season with salt and pepper, if necessary.

Serve the salad with the pitta crisps.

GET ORGANIZED
This salad can be partially assembled 3 hours beforehand, mash the feta but add the lemon, olive oil and red onion just before serving. The pitta crisps can be made the day before and stored in an airtight container.

Roasted baby courgettes, mint and bocconcini with sweet and sour vinaigrette

I tried this recipe many times using big courgettes and couldn't quite get it right. I rang my friend, Ursula Ferrigno, an Italian cookery writer, to find out why. "Never use courgettes wider than your thumb," she told me. The result — baby courgettes, baby creamy mozzarella and a drizzling of warm, sweet and sour vinaigrette — is superb.

SERVES 4/PREP 15 MINUTES/
COOK 10 MINUTES

500g/1lb 2oz baby courgettes (zucchini), cut in
  half or thirds lengthways
1 tbsp olive oil
250g/9oz bocconcini mozzarella (baby
  mozzarella), or 2 regular mozzarella cheeses,
  drained and cut into 2.5cm/1in chunks
2 tbsp toasted pine nuts
25 mint leaves
crusty bread, to serve

SWEET AND SOUR VINAIGRETTE
4 tbsp extra virgin olive oil
2 garlic cloves, thinly sliced
3 tbsp red wine vinegar
1 tsp dried red chilli flakes
1 tbsp clear honey
1 small red onion, thinly sliced
salt and freshly ground black pepper

Heat a griddle (grill) pan until very hot. Brush the courgettes with the olive oil and grill in batches until griddle marks appear on each side, about 1–2 minutes. Remove and place on a large platter and continue until all the courgettes are cooked.

To make the sweet and sour vinaigrette, heat the olive oil and garlic in a small pan until the garlic is golden, about 1 minute. Add the vinegar, chilli flakes, honey and onion, season with salt and pepper and simmer for 3–4 minutes until the mixture is syrupy. Remove from the heat and set aside.

Arrange the mozzarella on top of the courgettes. Spoon the warm vinaigrette over the salad and sprinkle with the pine nuts and mint leaves. Serve with crusty bread.

GET ORGANIZED
The dressing can be made and the courgettes grilled the morning of serving, and then refrigerated. Reheat the dressing just before serving and let the courgettes come back to room temperature.

Smoky aubergines with tomatoes and dill

Although blackening the aubergine over a hob (stovetop) flame can seem a little chaotic, it imparts a magical smokiness to this dip/salad. Serve with warm pitta bread or crunchy cos (romaine) lettuce.

SERVES 4/PREP 15 MINUTES/
COOK 15 MINUTES

3 large firm aubergines (eggplant)
2 large ripe plum tomatoes, de-seeded and diced
1 small red onion, finely chopped
3 garlic cloves, finely chopped
4 spring onions (scallions), thinly sliced
4 tbsp olive oil
1 tbsp lemon juice
1 tbsp finely chopped flat-leaf parsley leaves
1 tbsp finely chopped dill
salt and freshly ground black pepper

Pierce the whole aubergines in several places using the point of a sharp knife.

Using tongs, hold an aubergine over an open flame on the hob (stovetop). Turn it as it blackens and continue until charred all over. Repeat with the remaining aubergines. Alternatively, grill on a barbecue or under a preheated grill (broiler). Place the aubergines in a colander to drain off any excess liquid.

When the aubergines are cool enough to handle, carefully peel off the blackened skins and cut off the stalks. Remove any large seeds and roughly chop the flesh, then transfer to a large bowl.

Add the tomatoes, onion, garlic, spring onions, olive oil, lemon juice, parsley and dill. Season well with salt and pepper and gently combine.

GET ORGANIZED
The salad can be prepared 2 hours in advance, but don't add the onion until just before serving.

Greek salad

I discovered this wonderful salad while staying at a sunny villa in Crete. It contains the same ingredients as a Greek salad but instead of feta, it uses a creamy Myzithra cheese and is peppered with crisp aniseed croutons. Although I replaced them with goat's cheese and sourdough bread, its equally delicious.

SERVES 4/PREP 15 MINUTES

300g/10½oz cherry tomatoes, halved
1 small red onion, diced
4 Lebanese cucumbers, sliced, or 1 large
   cucumber, de-seeded and sliced
200g/7oz feta cheese, drained and cut into
   2.5cm/1in cubes
1 tbsp chopped fresh oregano or 1 tsp
   dried oregano
salt and freshly ground black pepper

ANCHOVY-CAPER DRESSING
1 anchovy in oil, rinsed and chopped
10 small capers in brine, rinsed and chopped
1 garlic clove, finely chopped
2 tbsp good-quality red wine vinegar, preferably
   Cabernet Sauvignon
4 tbsp extra virgin olive oil

To make the anchovy-caper dressing, put all the ingredients in a screw-top jar and shake well, then set aside.

Place the tomatoes, onion and cucumbers in a large serving bowl.

Just before serving, add the dressing, scatter over the feta and sprinkle with the oregano. Season to taste with salt and pepper, if necessary.

GET ORGANIZED
The vegetables and dressing can be assembled the morning of serving. Add the feta, dressing, oregano and salt and pepper shortly before serving.

Caponata

Sicilians are geniuses with aubergines, using them in practically everything. Caponata is like ratatouille, but a lush Italian version. Serve it warm or at room temperature with ricotta toasts.

SERVES 4/PREP 25 MINUTES/
COOK 30 MINUTES

3 aubergines (eggplant), cut into
   3cm/1¼in pieces
5 tbsp extra virgin olive oil
1 large onion, cut into 1cm/½in pieces
2 red (bell) peppers, de-seeded and cut into
   1cm/½in pieces
6 celery sticks, cut into 1cm/½in pieces
3 tbsp white wine vinegar
1 tbsp tomato purée (paste)
2 tbsp capers, rinsed
15 green olives, pitted (Sicilian Castelvetrano
   are perfect)
2 tbsp caster (superfine) sugar
salt and freshly ground black pepper

TOMATO SAUCE
3 tbsp olive oil
1 anchovy, rinsed
3 garlic cloves, finely chopped
500ml/17fl oz/2 cups passata (tomato purée)

RICOTTA TOASTS
100g/3½oz fresh ricotta cheese, drained
8 slices of bread, such as focaccia, toasted

Preheat the oven to 200°C/400°F/Gas Mark 6. Place the aubergines on a large baking (cookie) sheet, drizzle 4 tablespoons of the olive oil over them, sprinkle with a liberal amount of salt and pepper and mix well. Roast for 20 minutes, or until golden brown, shaking the baking sheet occasionally to prevent sticking. Set aside.

Meanwhile make the tomato sauce. Heat the olive oil in a saucepan, add the anchovy and garlic and sauté until the garlic is golden. Add the passata, salt and pepper and stir well. Cook over a medium-high heat for 15 minutes until thickened and reduced, then set aside.

Heat the remaining olive oil in a large sauté pan. Add the onion, red peppers and celery and season with salt and pepper, then sauté for 5 minutes until slightly soft, but still firm. Add the vinegar, tomato purée, capers, olives and tomato sauce and cook for 5 minutes. Remove from the heat and leave to cool. Add the roasted aubergines and gently mix.

Spread the ricotta over the toasts and serve with the caponata, either warm or at room temperature.

GET ORGANIZED
The entire salad can be made up to 4 days in advance – the flavour actually improves with time.

Saffron couscous with roasted vegetables and harissa dressing

Aromatic saffron couscous topped with sweet roasted vegetables, spicy harissa vinaigrette and a cool, refreshing yogurt sauce makes a one-dish meal that won't leave you disappointed.

SERVES 4/PREP 20 MINUTES/
COOK 30 MINUTES

1 tsp saffron threads, crushed
150ml/5fl oz/⅔ cup hot vegetable or
   chicken stock
250g/9oz/1⅓ cups couscous
1 tsp salt, plus extra for seasoning
700g/1lb 9oz sweet potatoes, peeled and cut
   into 1cm/½in chunks
4 red onions, cut into large chunks
3 red (bell) peppers, de-seeded and cut into
   large pieces
2 tbsp olive oil
1 handful of mint leaves, chopped
1 handful of coriander (cilantro) leaves, chopped
freshly ground black pepper

YOGURT SAUCE
200ml/7fl oz/scant 1 cup Greek (plain) yogurt
2 tbsp chopped mint leaves

HARISSA DRESSING
4 tbsp extra virgin olive oil
2 tsp harissa paste
1 garlic clove, crushed
½ tsp ground cumin
juice of 1 lemon
1 tbsp chopped flat-leaf parsley leaves
1 tsp clear honey

Preheat the oven to 200°C/400°F/Gas Mark 6.

Combine the saffron with the stock. Pour it over the couscous in a heatproof bowl, add the salt and mix well. Set aside, covered, for 10 minutes.

Arrange the sweet potatoes, onions and red peppers in a roasting pan, drizzle with the oil and season with salt and pepper. Roast for 30 minutes until golden and crisp.

Meanwhile make the harissa dressing. Put all the ingredients in a screw-top jar and shake well, then set aside.

To make the yogurt sauce, combine all the ingredients in a small bowl, stir to mix well, then chill in the refrigerator until required.

Break up the couscous with your fingers, making sure that there are no lumps, then tip it onto a large serving platter or into a large bowl. Place the roasted vegetables on top and pour the harissa dressing over. Sprinkle with the chopped mint and coriander and serve with the yogurt sauce on the side.

GET ORGANIZED
The dressing can be prepared the day before, but add the fresh herbs just before serving. The vegetables could be roasted up to 4 hours ahead, but may look less attractive than if prepared only 1–2 hours before.

Fattoush

Although every Middle Eastern country claims its own version, the Lebanese are the originators of this salad. Crispy pieces of pitta bread are tossed with crisp vegetables and a tart lemon and pomegranate dressing. It gets a final sprinkling of sumac, a purple-hued spice, which is slightly sour in taste.

SERVES 4/PREP 20 MINUTES/
COOK 10 MINUTES

1 cos (romaine) lettuce, cut into
   1cm/½in ribbons
200g/7oz cherry tomatoes, halved
4 spring onions (scallions), thinly sliced
4 Lebanese cucumbers, sliced, or 1 large
   cucumber, de-seeded and sliced
15 radishes, thinly sliced
1 red (bell) pepper, de-seeded and cut into
   1cm/½in dice
1 small handful of flat-leaf parsley leaves
15 mint leaves
1 tbsp ground sumac (optional)

POMEGRANATE AND LEMON DRESSING
5 tbsp pomegranate molasses
juice of ½ lemon
1 garlic clove, crushed
1 tsp sugar
3 tbsp extra virgin olive oil
½ tsp each salt and freshly ground black pepper

PITTA CROUTONS
6 pitta breads
3 tbsp extra virgin olive oil
1 tsp each salt and freshly ground black pepper

Preheat the oven to 200°C/400°F/Gas Mark 6. To make the pitta croûtons, spilt open and cut into 1cm/½in squares. Place the croûtons on a baking (cookie) sheet, drizzle with the olive oil and season with salt and pepper. Toss well and bake for 8 minutes or until golden. Leave to cool.

Meanwhile, make the pomegranate and lemon dressing. Put all the ingredients in a screw-top jar and shake well, then set aside.

Combine the lettuce, tomatoes, spring onions, cucumber, radishes, red pepper, parsley, mint and pitta croûtons in a large serving bowl.

Just before serving, pour the dressing over the salad and sprinkle with the sumac, if using.

GET ORGANIZED
The dressing can be made in the morning and the croûtons prepared a day ahead and stored in an airtight container. Add the croûtons and pour over the dressing just before serving.

Beefsteak tomatoes with spring onions and miso-ginger dressing

Miso, a fermented soybean paste from Japan, has a nutty, salty taste that can be used to make amazing dressings and marinades, or as a glaze for meat. Not only packed with umami vour, it has numerous health benefits – a great bonus. It's sold in most supermarkets or health food stores.

SERVES 4/PREP 15 MINUTES

4 large ripe red or yellow beefsteak tomatoes, cut
  into thick slices
200g/7oz cherry tomatoes, halved
4 spring onions (scallions), julienned or chopped
1 large handful of mizuna or rocket
  (arugula) leaves
1 tbsp black or white sesame seeds

MISO-GINGER DRESSING
2 tbsp pale (shiro) miso paste
3 tbsp mirin
1 tbsp sugar
juice of ½ lemon
2 tbsp rice wine vinegar
1 tsp Japanese soy sauce
1 tbsp finely grated fresh root ginger

To make the miso-ginger dressing, combine the ingredients in a screw-top jar and shake well, then set aside.

Arrange the tomato slices and cherry tomatoes, spring onions and mizuna on a large platter.

Pour the dressing over the salad and sprinkle with the sesame seeds. Serve immediately.

GET ORGANIZED
The dressing can be made in the morning and the salad prepared a couple of hours before serving. Keep the spring onions aside until just before serving.

Chickpea, chorizo and pepper salad with sherry-mustard vinaigrette

Crispy slices of chorizo, smoky roasted peppers and sharp sherry vinegar makes this a stellar salad. Spanish piquillo peppers have a particular smoky flavour that is a step up from regular jarred varieties. If you can't find them, simply substitute roasted red peppers.

SERVES 4/PREP 10 MINUTES/
COOK 10 MINUTES

400g/14oz fresh chorizo sausage, cut into
  1cm/½in thick slices
2 x 400g/14oz cans chickpeas (garbanzo beans),
  drained and rinsed, or 250g/9oz/1¼ cups
  dried chickpeas, soaked overnight and boiled
  for 1–2 hours until soft, drained (page 7)
200g/7oz piquillo or other roasted (bell)
  peppers, cut into 2.5cm/1in squares
2 small shallots, finely diced
25g/1oz flat-leaf parsley, leaves finely chopped
freshly ground black pepper

SHERRY-MUSTARD VINAIGRETTE
2 tbsp sherry vinegar
4 tbsp extra virgin olive oil
1 tsp Dijon mustard
½ tsp salt, plus extra for seasoning
2 tsp clear honey

Heat a large, dry, non-stick frying pan until hot. Add the chorizo slices and cook, in batches, until crisp and browned all over. Drain the chorizo on kitchen paper (paper towels).

To make the sherry-mustard vinaigrette, put all the ingredients in a screw-top jar and shake well, then set aside.

Combine the chickpeas, piquillo peppers, shallots, parsley and cooked chorizo in a medium serving bowl.

Just before serving, pour the dressing over the salad and mix gently. Taste for seasoning and add salt and pepper, if necessary.

GET ORGANIZED
The dressing can be made the day before and the salad ingredients can be assembled up to 6 hours before serving.

Borlotti beans with tuna, celery and lemon and olive oil dressing

I love making this for a quick lunch as most of the ingredients are usually in my store cupboard (pantry) or refrigerator. If you've never had canned Italian or Spanish tuna packed in olive oil, you are in for a great surprise. Although not expensive, it is miles beyond the often banal supermarket varieties. The rich, silky tuna is a perfect partner for the creamy borlotti beans and tart lemon dressing.

SERVES 4/PREP 15 MINUTES

2 x 400g/14oz cans borlotti (cranberry) beans, drained and rinsed
2 celery hearts (the inner part of the celery heads) with leaves, thinly sliced
1 small red onion, finely chopped
1 large handful of flat-leaf parsley, finely chopped
250g/9oz can Italian or Spanish tuna in olive oil, drained
2 hard-boiled (hard-cooked) eggs, peeled and quartered

LEMON AND OLIVE OIL DRESSING

juice of 1 lemon
½ tsp grated lemon zest
5 tbsp extra virgin olive oil
1 tbsp clear honey
½ tsp each salt and freshly ground black pepper, plus extra for seasoning

To make the lemon and olive oil dressing, put all the ingredients in a screw-top jar and shake well, then set aside.

Combine the beans, celery, onion and parsley in a medium bowl.

Pour the dressing over the salad, stir until combined, then transfer it to a shallow serving dish. Arrange the tuna and eggs on top, check the seasoning and serve.

Tip: To cook a hard-boiled egg, bring a small pan of water to the boil. Add a medium-sized egg, at room temperature, and boil for 7 minutes. For soft-boiled, cook the egg for 6 minutes. If your eggs are especially large, then cook for an extra minute for either preference. Remove from the water and run under cold water until completely cool. Peel just before slicing.

GET ORGANIZED

The dressing and whole eggs can be made the day before. The salad can be prepared up to 4 hours before serving and stored in the refrigerator. It may be wise to keep the onion separate, so it doesn't overpower the other flavours.

Moroccan carrots

This classic North African carrot salad is a great addition to a meze menu. The carrots are blanched and then marinated in a zesty vinaigrette of paprika, parsley and garlic. It keeps for up to a week refrigerated, so save any leftovers to pack in your lunchbox with some bulgar wheat or quinoa.

SERVES 4/PREP 20 MINUTES/
COOK 5 MINUTES

750g/1lb 10oz carrots, sliced into 3cm/1¼in
  pieces
100g/3½oz thick Greek yogurt (optional)

SPICED VINAIGRETTE
3 tbsp extra virgin olive oil
3 tbsp red wine vinegar, preferably Cabernet
  Sauvignon
1½ tsp sweet paprika, preferably pimentón
1½ tsp ground cumin
2 garlic cloves, finely chopped
1 handful of flat-leaf parsley, finely chopped
salt and freshly ground black pepper

To make the spiced vinaigrette, mix together the olive oil, vinegar, paprika, cumin, garlic, parsley and some salt and pepper in a medium bowl, then set aside.

Cook the carrots in a large pan of salted boiling water until tender, but still firm, about 2 minutes. Overcooking will produce a slimy texture so drain them immediately they are al dente.

Toss the warm carrots in the vinaigrette and leave at room temperature until ready to serve, or chill overnight.

To serve, smear a large tablespoon of Greek yogurt, if using, over each serving plate and top with the dressed carrots.

GET ORGANIZED
Make the entire salad up to 24 hours in advance and store in the refrigerator.

Tabbouleh with preserved lemon

This ubiquitous Middle Eastern meze salad hails from Lebanon. Don't be alarmed at the quantity of parsley called for here, the ratio of the herb to wheat is traditional. Although any cucumber could be used, Lebanese cucumbers are preferred for their intense aroma and crunchy texture, and are far less watery than their unexceptional hothouse cousins. They are easily found in Middle Eastern stores. Preserved lemons are pickled in salt and sugar, which tames their bitterness and concentrates their citrus intensity.

SERVES 4/PREP 35 MINUTES

200g/7oz/heaped 1 cup fine bulgar wheat
juice of 2 lemons, plus extra if needed
125ml/4fl oz/½ cup extra virgin olive oil
1 tsp salt, plus extra for seasoning
4 small Lebanese cucumbers, or 2 medium
   cucumbers
1 large red onion, finely diced
1 tsp ground cumin
½ tsp ground cinnamon
5 plum tomatoes, de-seeded and finely diced
1 large bunch of flat-leaf parsley, leaves
   finely chopped
1 bunch of mint, leaves finely chopped
6 spring onions (scallions), thinly sliced
1 large or 2 small preserved lemons, rind only,
   chopped

Place the bulgar in a medium bowl and cover with the lemon juice and olive oil, season with salt and leave to soak for 30 minutes.

Meanwhile, chop the cucumber into dice or thin slices. If using a hothouse cucumber, you will want to remove the seeds first with a teaspoon.

Add the remaining ingredients to a large bowl. Tip in the lemon-soaked bulgar wheat, toss well, taste, and add more lemon juice or salt, if necessary.

GET ORGANIZED
This salad will keep for up to 48 hours in the refrigerator, but is best eaten within 24 hours.

Rosemary cannellini beans with parmesan and roasted cherry tomatoes

Cannellini beans with their creamy yet firm texture make an ideal base for a salad. The soffritto, made with garlic, onion and rosemary, bumps up the depth of flavour, while the roasted tomatoes, crisp red onion and Parmesan make it even more memorable.

SERVES 4/PREP 10 MINUTES/
COOK 15 MINUTES

250g/9oz cherry tomatoes, halved
4 tbsp olive oil
3 garlic cloves, chopped
1 large red onion, finely chopped
2 tsp chopped rosemary
2 x 400g/14oz cans cannellini beans, drained
  and rinsed
5 tbsp balsamic vinegar
60g/2¼oz Parmesan cheese, coarsely grated
  or shaved
salt and freshly ground black pepper

Preheat the oven to 190°C/375°F/Gas Mark 5. Place the cherry tomatoes, cut-side up, on a baking (cookie) sheet, drizzle with 1 tablespoon of the olive oil and roast for 15 minutes until softened. Remove them from the sheet and set aside.

Meanwhile, heat the remaining olive oil in a large frying pan. Add the garlic, onion and rosemary, season to taste with salt and pepper and cook over a low heat for about 6 minutes until softened.

Add the cannellini beans and vinegar and cook until the beans are heated through.

Stir in the Parmesan and tip the warm salad into a serving platter or bowl. Top with the roasted tomatoes and serve.

GET ORGANIZED
The salad is warm so it is best cooked and eaten straight away.

Tomato, sourdough croûton and parmesan salad with balsamic dressing

Tomatoes abound in late summer and this salad celebrates their sweet taste. Even in the winter, you can make this with cherry tomatoes and it's delicious. It's a bit like a bowl of tomato bruschetta tossed together, but better. For the ultimate croûtons, use sourdough bread – it retains its crunch even after soaking up the wonderful balsamic dressing.

SERVES 4/PREP 15 MINUTES/
COOK 10 MINUTES

200g/7oz sourdough bread, cut into
    2cm/¾in cubes
2 tbsp extra virgin olive oil
500g/1lb 2oz ripe cherry tomatoes, halved, or 6
    plum tomatoes, de-seeded and roughly chopped
2 tbsp diced red onion
5 tbsp coarsely grated Parmesan cheese
1 large bunch of basil, leaves roughly chopped
freshly ground black pepper

BALSAMIC DRESSING
3 tbsp good-quality balsamic vinegar
5 tbsp extra virgin olive oil
1 garlic clove, finely chopped
1 tsp Dijon mustard
1 tsp sugar
½ tsp salt, plus extra for seasoning

Preheat the oven to 200°C/400°F/Gas Mark 6. Place the bread cubes on a large baking (cookie) sheet. Toss them in the oil and season well with salt and pepper. Bake for 8–9 minutes or until golden, then leave to cool.

Meanwhile, make the balsamic dressing. Put all the ingredients in a screw-top jar and shake well, then set aside.

In a large bowl, mix together the tomatoes, onion, Parmesan, basil and sourdough croûtons. Just before serving, pour the dressing over the salad and mix again.

GET ORGANIZED
The croûtons can be made 2 days in advance and stored in an airtight container. The dressing can be prepared the day before. The salad can be made in the morning, but keep the onion separate until serving.

Tomato, asparagus and gorgonzola salad

In spring, nothing beats tender spears of asparagus blanched to perfection. Gorgonzola cheese, lemon vinaigrette and tomatoes are scattered over for an Italian-inspired salad. If you can't find worthy standard tomatoes, try using quartered cherry tomatoes.

**SERVES 4/PREP 15 MINUTES/
COOK 5 MINUTES**

500g/1lb 2oz asparagus spears, trimmed
5 plum or vine-ripened tomatoes, de-seeded
   and diced
1 garlic clove, finely chopped
2 shallots, finely chopped
1 large bunch of basil, leaves finely shredded
75g/2½oz Gorgonzola or Roquefort cheese,
   crumbled

LEMON VINAIGRETTE
juice of ½ lemon
4 tbsp extra virgin olive oil
½ tsp salt, plus extra for seasoning
freshly ground black pepper

To make the lemon vinaigrette, put all the ingredients in a screw-top jar, season with the salt and some pepper and shake well, then set aside.

Blanch the asparagus in a large pan of salted boiling water until al dente, about 1 minute. Drain and immediately immerse in iced water to prevent any further cooking (this keeps the asparagus bright green). Drain again and dry on clean tea towels (dish towels).

Place the tomatoes in a medium bowl and add the lemon vinaigrette, garlic, shallots and basil. Season to taste with salt and pepper, if needed. Turn until combined, then set aside.

Arrange the asparagus on a large platter or individual serving plates. Spoon the tomato mixture over and place the crumbled cheese on top before serving.

GET ORGANIZED
The dressing can be prepared the day before. The asparagus can be blanched and the tomato mixture can be made up to 6 hours in advance, but add the basil, shallot and the dressing just before serving.

Saffron patatas aioli

Tapas are not just a snack, they can make a distinctive meal of their own. Ranging from leeks in vinaigrette to a humble seared chorizo sausage, they are bursting with flavour. Serve this garlicky potato salad with small plates of salted Marcona almonds, slices of chorizo, black pitted olives, Manchego cheese and, of course, an obligatory glass of sherry.

SERVES 4/PREP 20 MINUTES/
COOK 20 MINUTES

Saffron Aioli (see page 77)
5 medium to large red potatoes, such as a Maris
   Piper or other creamy variety, unpeeled
1 tbsp sherry vinegar
1 large bunch of chives, finely chopped
salt

Follow the instructions for making the Saffron Aioli on page 77.

Cook the potatoes in a large pan of salted boiling water until tender, about 10 minutes or until tender when cut with a knife. Drain and leave to cool slightly, then peel the potatoes and cut into 2cm/¾in cubes.

Sprinkle the potatoes with a good amount of salt (potatoes need a lot) and the sherry vinegar. Gently toss together and chill until the potatoes are cold.

When cool, gently mix the potatoes in a serving bowl with the aioli. Sprinkle with the chives and serve.

GET ORGANIZED
The potato salad can be prepared and refrigerated the morning of serving. It will keep for up to 2–3 days refrigerated, but the garlic will continue to get stronger. Sprinkle with chives just before serving.

Baby lettuce with chicken, raspberry and walnut oil vinaigrette and Parmesan tuiles

Delicate Parmesan tuiles make any bowl of lettuce instantly more glamorous. They sound complicated but they are simply grated Parmesan baked into a lacy wafer. The dressing is also key; the mixture of balsamic and raspberry vinegars and nut oil makes a top-shelf vinaigrette.

SERVES 4/PREP 20 MINUTES/
COOK 30 MINUTES

50g/1¾oz Parmesan cheese, finely grated
1 tsp extra virgin olive oil
2 boneless chicken breasts with skin on
4 large handfuls of mesclun (mixed young lettuce
    leaves), about 100g/3½oz total weight
200g/7oz raspberries
4 spring onions (scallions), white part only,
    thinly sliced

RASPBERRY AND WALNUT OIL VINAIGRETTE

4 tbsp raspberry vinegar
2 tbsp balsamic vinegar
4 tbsp extra virgin olive oil
3 tbsp walnut or hazelnut oil
1 tsp Dijon mustard
freshly ground black pepper

CARAMELIZED WALNUTS

50g/1¾oz/½ cup walnut halves
2 tbsp clear honey
½ tsp salt, plus extra for seasoning
1 tbsp caster (superfine) sugar
2 tsp vegetable oil

Preheat the oven to 200°C/400°F/Gas Mark 6. Line a baking (cookie) sheet with non-stick baking paper. It's very important that the paper is silicone treated or non-stick as the Parmesan tuiles can be difficult to remove from ordinary parchment baking paper.

To make the Parmesan tuiles, sprinkle the cheese into 8 x 8cm/3in rounds. Keep them flat and not too thick in the middle. Bake for 6–7 minutes or until golden brown and bubbly. Leave to cool on the sheet.

Meanwhile, make the caramelized walnuts. Toss the walnuts with the other ingredients on a separate baking sheet and bake for 6 minutes. Transfer to a non-stick baking paper and leave to crisp up.

Heat the oil in a small ovenproof frying pan. Place the chicken skin-side down and sear until golden, about 5 minutes. Turn over and sear on the other side. Place the chicken in the preheated oven to finish off cooking for another 5 minutes, or until cooked through. Remove and leave to rest for 5 minutes, then slice into thick pieces.

While the chicken is cooking, make the raspberry and walnut oil vinaigrette. Put all the ingredients in a screw-top jar, season with salt and pepper and shake well, then set aside.

Place the lettuce leaves on individual plates or a large platter and arrange the raspberries, spring onions, chicken and caramelized walnuts on top. Pour the dressing over and top each plate with 2 Parmesan tuiles.

GET ORGANIZED
The dressing can be prepared the day before and refrigerated. The nuts and Parmesan tuiles can also be made a day ahead and stored in airtight containers.

Balsamic fig, prosciutto and ricotta crostini with rocket salad

My great friend Victoria and I ate this delicious salad in an Italian trattoria in Toronto. Baby figs are boiled and then simmered in balsamic vinegar. The syrupy, sweet and sour fruit is arranged on ricotta crostini and served with peppery rocket leaves.

SERVES 4/PREP 10 MINUTES/
COOK 25 MINUTES

16 dried baby-sized figs or 8 regular-sized ones
125ml/4fl oz/½ cup balsamic vinegar, plus extra
   for drizzling
125ml/4fl oz/½ cup water
1 tbsp sugar
1 tsp salt
½ tsp freshly ground black pepper, plus extra
   for seasoning
2 large handfuls of rocket (arugula) leaves
100g/3½oz full-fat ricotta cheese, drained
8 slices of ciabatta or sourdough, toasted and
   brushed with olive oil
4 slices of prosciutto or serrano ham

Place the figs in a small pan, add water to cover and bring to the boil. Turn the heat down and simmer for 10 minutes, then drain.

Bring the balsamic vinegar and measured water to the boil with the sugar, salt and pepper. Add the figs, turn the heat down and simmer for 15 minutes or until the vinegar is syrupy and the figs are reconstituted. Leave to cool slightly.

Arrange the rocket on individual plates or a large dish. Spread the ricotta over the toasted slices of bread and place 2 on each plate. Top each crostini with a spoonful of the figs and syrup, then drizzle some over the rocket.

Twist the slices of prosciutto and place 1 on each plate. Grind extra black pepper over and drizzle with any remaining syrup.

GET ORGANIZED
Toast the bread 2 days ahead of serving and store in an airtight container. Prepare the figs a day in advance and reheat before making the salad. Assemble the crostini just before serving.

Grilled courgette and pepper salad with feta, mint and balsamic dressing

This recipe was inspired by Sophie Grigson's book, *Eat Your Greens*. Grilled courgettes and roasted peppers are tossed in a garlicky balsamic dressing while still warm and then sprinkled with feta cheese and fresh mint. It's wonderful served warm in the winter or refreshing at room temperature in the summer months.

SERVES 4/PREP 15 MINUTES/
COOK 15 MINUTES

4 red (bell) peppers, de-seeded and quartered
4 courgettes (zucchini), cut lengthways into
   1cm/½in thick slices
4 tbsp olive oil
2 tbsp chopped mint, leaves
200g/7oz feta cheese, drained and crumbled

BALSAMIC DRESSING
5 tbsp good-quality balsamic vinegar
125ml/4fl oz/½ cup extra virgin olive oil
1 garlic clove, finely chopped
1 tsp Dijon mustard
1 tsp sugar
1 tsp salt, plus extra for seasoning
½ tsp freshly ground black pepper, plus extra
   for seasoning

Preheat the grill (broiler) to high. Arrange the red peppers, skin-side up, in a large roasting pan. Place under the grill and cook until blackened, then transfer to a plastic bag and seal. Set aside for 5 minutes.

Place the courgettes in the same pan. Toss with the olive oil and sprinkle with salt and pepper. Place under the grill and cook, turning once, until both sides are golden. (Alternatively, you can use a griddle (grill) pan to grill the courgettes.) Remove the courgettes from the pan and place in a large serving bowl.

While the vegetables are cooking, make the balsamic dressing. Put all the ingredients in a screw-top jar and shake well, then set aside.

When the peppers are cool enough to handle, remove the skins but do not rinse. Cut the flesh into large pieces. Add them to the courgettes in the bowl.

Pour the dressing over the vegetables while they are still warm and sprinkle the mint on top. Just before serving, scatter over the feta.

If serving hot, you could place everything in an ovenproof dish under the grill and briefly brown the cheese.

GET ORGANIZED
The vegetables can be grilled in the morning and the dressing made the day ahead. If preparing in advance, pour only half of the dressing over the warm vegetables, then add the mint, feta and remaining dressing just before serving.

Warm salad of green beans and poached egg with ravigote dressing

I used to live near a sweet French brasserie called Brula. This was one of its signature dishes, and it's perfect for brunch or a simple lunch or dinner.

SERVES 4/PREP 10 MINUTES/
COOK 20 MINUTES

4 free-range eggs
1 litre/1¾ pints/4 cups water
1 tbsp white wine vinegar
300g/10½oz green beans, trimmed
1 tbsp olive oil

RAVIGOTE DRESSING
2 tsp Dijon mustard
1 tbsp red wine vinegar
3 tbsp extra virgin olive oil
1 tbsp small capers, rinsed and chopped
1 tbsp finely chopped flat-leaf parsley leaves
1 tbsp finely chopped tarragon leaves
1 tbsp finely chopped shallot
salt and freshly ground black pepper

To make the ravigote dressing, whisk together the mustard, vinegar and some salt and pepper in a small bowl. Gradually whisk in the oil. Stir in the capers, herbs and shallot, then set aside.

To make the perfect poached egg, break an egg into a fine-mesh sieve (strainer) and let any excess liquid drain off, then slide it into a bowl. Bring the measured water to the boil in a shallow saucepan with the vinegar. Swirl the boiling water with a spoon, gently slide the egg into the centre of the swirling water and poach for 3–5 minutes until the white is set and the yolk remains runny. Carefully remove with a slotted spoon and drain on a clean tea towel (dish towel). Repeat with the remaining eggs.

While the eggs are poaching, blanch the beans in a pan of salted boiling water until al dente, about 1 minute. Drain and immediately immerse in iced water (this will help retain the green colour of the beans). Drain again and set aside.

Just before serving, gently reheat the beans in the olive oil. Divide the beans among individual serving plates, place a poached egg on each and drizzle the dressing over.

GET ORGANIZED
The beans and dressing can both be prepared the morning of serving, but bear in mind that the dressing loses its green colour if kept for longer than 3–4 hours.

Panzanella salad

There are a lot of ingredients in this classic Tuscan salad but it's worth every second of chopping. I love the different textures of crunchy croûtons with soft tomatoes and crisp cucumber and peppers. The capers and olives add a salty pop to every bite.

SERVES 4/PREP 20 MINUTES/
COOK 15 MINUTES

1 ciabatta or sourdough loaf, cut into
  1cm/½in cubes
2 red (bell) peppers, de-seeded and quartered
250g/9oz cherry tomatoes, halved
1 celery heart, (the inner part of the celery
  head), sliced
10 Italian black olives, pitted and halved
2 tbsp small capers, rinsed
1 small red onion, finely diced
2–3 mini cucumbers, peeled and sliced, or
  1 medium cucumber, peeled, de-seeded
  and sliced
20 basil leaves, shredded
1 anchovy, rinsed and chopped
1 garlic clove, finely chopped
4 tbsp extra virgin olive oil
4 tbsp good-quality red wine vinegar, preferably
  Cabernet Sauvignon
salt and freshly ground black pepper

Preheat the oven to 200°C/400°F/Gas Mark 6. Spread out the bread cubes on a baking (cookie) sheet and toast in the oven for 5 minutes or until crisp. Remove from the oven and leave to cool.

Preheat the grill (broiler) to high. Place the peppers, skin-side up, on a large baking sheet and grill (broil) until blackened. Place the peppers in a plastic bag, seal and set aside for 5 minutes.

When the peppers are cool enough to handle, remove the skins but do not rinse. Thinly slice the flesh and place in a large bowl. Add the tomatoes, celery, olives, capers, onion, cucumbers, basil, anchovy, garlic and croûtons to the bowl.

Just before serving, drizzle the oil and vinegar over the salad, season with plenty of salt and pepper and toss until combined and serve.

GET ORGANIZED
The salad ingredients can be assembled the day before, keeping the garlic, onion, anchovy, basil, croûtons, oil and vinegar separate, then mix together just before serving.

Red oak leaf lettuce with crispy prosciutto, gorgonzola and honey-mustard dressing

We all have our everyday 'go-to' mixed salad and I'd like to think that this one could become your new favourite. Mild lettuces are tossed in a sweet honey-mustard dressing and then showered with prosciutto and Gorgonzola for a crazy-good combination.

SERVES 4/PREP 15 MINUTES/
COOK 5 MINUTES

1 red oak leaf lettuce, torn into
   2.5cm/1in pieces
½ round (butterhead) lettuce, torn into
   2.5cm/1in pieces
2–3 radicchio leaves, torn into 2.5cm/1in pieces
1 red (bell) pepper, de-seeded and cut into
   thin batons
2 small celery sticks (heart only), cut into
   thin slices
200g/7oz cherry tomatoes, halved
2 small red onions, cut into thin rings
a little vegetable oil, for frying
6 slices of prosciutto
125g/4½oz Gorgonzola cheese, crumbled

HONEY-MUSTARD DRESSING
5 tbsp light olive oil
1½ tbsp red wine vinegar
1 tbsp Dijon mustard
1 tbsp clear honey
½ garlic clove, finely chopped
½ tsp each salt and freshly ground
   black pepper

Place both types of lettuce and the radicchio leaves in a large bowl. Add the red pepper, celery, tomatoes and onions and set aside.

Heat a lightly oiled frying pan over a medium heat and cook the prosciutto until crispy, about 3–4 minutes. Leave to cool and then break into tiny pieces. Add to the salad.

To make the honey-mustard dressing, put all the ingredients in a screw-top jar and shake well, then set aside.

Just before serving, pour the dressing over the salad and top with the Gorgonzola.

GET ORGANIZED
The dressing can be made up to 24 hours ahead. The salad can be assembled in the morning and stored in the refrigerator, but do not add the onions, prosciutto, Gorgonzola and dressing until just before serving.

Farmer's market salad with croûtons and goat's cheese

While staying at a sunny villa in Crete, this salad, made with aniseed crackers, creamy Myzithra cheese and Greek salad-type ingredients, became a favourite. I've tried to replicate it and although the goat's cheese and sourdough croûtons have replaced the authentic originals, the result is not far off.

SERVES 4/PREP 15 MINUTES/
COOK 8 MINUTES

5 slices of sourdough bread, cut into
  2cm/¾in cubes
2 tbsp olive oil
300g/10½oz ripe cherry tomatoes, halved
1 small red onion, finely chopped
3 small Lebanese cucumbers, sliced, or 1 large
  cucumber, peeled and sliced
10 black olives in oil, drained and pitted
2 tbsp chopped fresh oregano or
  2 tsp dried oregano
150g/5½oz mild goat's cheese, crumbled
salt

ANCHOVY, CAPER AND GARLIC DRESSING
1 anchovy in oil, rinsed and chopped
10 small capers in brine, rinsed and chopped
1 garlic clove, finely chopped
½ tsp freshly ground black pepper, plus extra
  for seasoning
3 tbsp good-quality red wine vinegar, preferably
  Cabernet Sauvignon
4 tbsp extra virgin olive oil

Preheat the oven to 200°C/400°F/Gas Mark 6. Spread out the bread cubes on a baking (cookie) sheet, toss with the olive oil, season with salt and pepper, then bake for 8 minutes until golden and crisp. Leave to cool.

Meanwhile make the anchovy, caper and garlic dressing. Put all the ingredients in a screw-top jar and shake well, then set aside.

Put the tomatoes, onion, cucumbers, olives and oregano in a large serving bowl with the croûtons.

Just before serving, add the dressing to the salad and mix well. Scatter the goat's cheese over the top and serve.

GET ORGANIZED
The croûtons can be prepared 2 days ahead and stored in an airtight container. The dressing can be prepared the day before. The salad can be prepared on the day, but add the onion just before serving.

Chicory, roquefort and pear salad with walnut oil vinaigrette

This classic bistro salad is the perfect partner to roast meat or chicken. The combination of bitter leaves, sweet pear and salty cheese makes a simple but delicious salad.

SERVES 4/PREP 15 MINUTES

3 heads of red or white chicory (Belgian endive), trimmed and sliced into 2.5cm/1in pieces
100g/3½oz baby watercress leaves
2 ripe pears, cored and chopped into 2cm/¾in pieces
juice of ½ lemon
50g/1¾oz/½ cup pecans, chopped
75g/2½oz/¾ cup crumbled Roquefort or Gorgonzola, or other piquant blue cheese

WALNUT OIL VINAIGRETTE
3 tbsp sherry vinegar
4 tbsp walnut or hazelnut oil
½ tsp Dijon mustard
1 tsp sugar
½ tsp salt

To make the walnut oil vinaigrette, put all the ingredients in a screw-top jar and shake well, then set aside.

Place the chicory in a large salad bowl with the watercress.

Toss the pears with the lemon juice in a separate bowl to stop them discoloring and set aside.

Just before serving, add the pears, nuts, cheese and dressing to the salad bowl and toss well.

GET ORGANIZED
The dressing can be made the day before. Assemble the other ingredients shortly before serving.

ocket, avocado and palm heart salad with lemon and olive oil dressing

In Florence's Trattoria Garga, owned by an artist-husband and chef-wife, beautiful murals provide a stunning backdrop for unbelievable food. This is their house salad – it includes palm hearts, a South American ingredient, which was delightfully unexpected in Italy.

SERVES 4/PREP 10 MINUTES

1 avocado, peeled, stoned (pitted), and
  roughly diced
½ lemon
3 large bunches of rocket (arugula) leaves
1 small head of radicchio, torn into small pieces
250g/9oz cherry tomatoes, halved
6 palm hearts, cut into 1cm/½in slices
60g/2¼oz/½ cup toasted pine nuts
60g/2¼oz Parmesan cheese, coarsely grated

LEMON AND OLIVE OIL DRESSING
juice of 1 lemon
½ tsp grated lemon zest
4 tbsp extra virgin olive oil
1 tbsp clear honey
½ tsp each salt and freshly ground black pepper

To make the lemon and olive oil dressing, put all the ingredients in a screw-top jar and shake well, then set aside.

Place the avocado in a bowl, add a squeeze of lemon juice to prevent it discoloring and set aside.

Combine the rocket, radicchio, tomatoes, palm hearts, pine nuts and Parmesan in a separate bowl.

Just before serving, add the avocado to the salad and pour the dressing over. Mix well and serve immediately.

GET ORGANIZED
The dressing can be made the day before. The salad can be prepared in the morning and refrigerated, do not include the avocado until just before serving.

Roasted baby beetroot with warm goat's cheese cakes

My husband, a sworn beetroot hater, was finally converted when I made this dish. Baby beetroots are much sweeter than their larger counterparts so do seek them out, if you can. The warm crispy goat's cheese cakes benefit from freezing before pan-frying, otherwise they start to melt too quickly.

SERVES 4/PREP 15 MINUTES, PLUS FREEZING/COOK 30 MINUTES

12 raw red or yellow baby beetroots (beets) or 4 medium beetroots, well scrubbed, halved or quartered depending on size
4 tbsp olive oil
125g/4½oz/2 cups dry sourdough or panko breadcrumbs
1 egg, beaten
4 small goat's cheese crottins, about 3cm/1¼in thick
4 handfuls of rocket (arugula) leaves
salt and freshly ground black pepper

BALSAMIC DRESSING
3 tbsp good-quality balsamic vinegar
4 tbsp extra virgin olive oil
1 garlic clove, finely chopped
1 tsp Dijon mustard
1 tsp sugar

Preheat the oven to 200°C/400°F/Gas Mark 6. Put the beetroots on a large piece of foil, drizzle with half of the oil and season with salt and pepper. Close the foil parcel, place on a baking (cookie) sheet and roast for 15 minutes. Open the foil parcel and cook for another 10 minutes or until the beetroots are tender.

Meanwhile, place the breadcrumbs in a shallow bowl. Beat the egg in another bowl. Dip the cheese rounds into the beaten egg, then roll them in the breadcrumbs until coated. Chill in the freezer for at least 20 minutes until firmed up.

To make the balsamic dressing, put all the ingredients in a screw-top jar and shake well, then set aside.

When the beetroot is cooked, arrange on individual serving plates and top with the rocket.

Heat the remaining olive oil in a large frying pan and fry the goat's cheese cakes for about 1 minute on each side or until golden. By the time you finish cooking the second side, the cheese will be melting.

Place a cheese cake on each plate, drizzle the dressing over and serve immediately.

Tip: If you can't find thin goat's cheese crottins then buy 2 thick ones and cut in half crossways.

GET ORGANIZED
The beetroot tastes best prepared on the day of serving, but it could be roasted the day before. The goat's cheese cakes and dressing can be prepared the day before and stored separately in the refrigerator.

orange, asparagus and halloumi salad with citrus caper vinaigrette

Halloumi, a salty rubbery Cypriot cheese, is ideal for chargrilling or pan-frying. Its plain taste teams beautifully with any piquant dressing.

SERVES 4/PREP 15 MINUTES/ COOK 5 MINUTES

1 large bunch of thin asparagus, trimmed
3 blood or navel oranges
2 tbsp olive oil
2 x 200g/7oz blocks halloumi cheese, drained, patted dry and cut into 16 slices

CITRUS CAPER VINAIGRETTE

2 tbsp capers, rinsed and chopped
1 garlic clove, finely chopped
1 small shallot, finely chopped
3 tbsp finely chopped flat-leaf parsley leaves
1 tbsp grainy French mustard
1 tbsp orange juice
2 tbsp red wine vinegar
3 tbsp extra virgin olive oil
salt and freshly ground black pepper

To make the caper vinaigrette, put all the ingredients in a screw-top jar, season with salt and pepper and shake well, then set aside.

Blanch the asparagus in a pan of salted boiling water until al dente, about 1 minute. Drain and immediately immerse in iced water. Drain again and set aside.

Slice off the rind from the oranges and cut the flesh into thick slices. Set aside.

Heat the olive oil in a sauté pan until very hot. Brown the halloumi until crispy on both sides, about 2 minutes.

Divide the halloumi among individual plates. Arrange the asparagus and oranges over the top.

Drizzle the vinaigrette over the salad and serve immediately.

GET ORGANIZED
The asparagus, orange slices and vinaigrette can be prepared in the morning. The halloumi should not be fried until just before serving.

Crispy aubergine, spring onion and chilli salad with sweet soy and lime dressing

After a brilliant lunch at E&O restaurant in Notting Hill, London, I was spurred into making my own version of their exalted aubergine salad with soy. I found frying the aubergine wasn't necessary and grilling produced an equally tasty and healthier result.

SERVES 4/PREP 15 MINUTES/
COOK 10 MINUTES

4 spring onions (scallions), cut into thin julienne
2 thumb-sized red chillies, de-seeded and cut
   into thin julienne
3 small to medium aubergines (eggplant), cut
   into 2.5cm/1in thick slices
3–4 tbsp groundnut (peanut) or vegetable oil
1 small handful of coriander (cilantro) leaves
salt and freshly ground black pepper

SWEET SOY AND LIME DRESSING
5 tbsp kecap manis (sweet soy sauce)
2 thumb-sized red chillies, de-seeded
   and chopped
1 garlic clove, finely chopped
1 tbsp finely chopped fresh root ginger
juice of 2 limes
1 tbsp caster (superfine) sugar

Place the spring onions and chillies in wet kitchen paper (paper towels) and chill in the refrigerator until required. This makes them crisp and sweeter in taste.

To make the soy and lime dressing, put all the ingredients in a small bowl and mix well. Alternatively, pulse them in a food processor. Set aside.

Brush both sides of the aubergine slices liberally with the oil. Season with salt and pepper. Heat a griddle (grill) pan and grill the aubergines in batches for about 1–2 minutes on each side or until griddle marks appear. Remove to a platter and continue to grill the remaining aubergines.

Pour the dressing over the salad, sprinkle with the spring onions, chillies and coriander and serve immediately.

GET ORGANIZED
The dressing can be made the day before, but the salad should be served within 2 hours of preparation.

Warm baby artichokes with cherry tomatoes and olives

I discovered this recipe at Roger Vergé's cooking school in Mougins, southern France. The artichokes are bathed in a sauce of mirepoix, red wine vinegar, honey and fresh herbs. Baby artichokes are easiest to use as their undeveloped chokes just need a little trimming.

SERVES 4/PREP 30 MINUTES/
COOK 25 MINUTES

2 lemons, halved
16 baby artichokes
1 large onion, finely chopped
1 large carrot, finely chopped
4 garlic cloves, finely chopped
3 tbsp olive oil
3 tbsp red wine vinegar
2 tbsp clear honey
250ml/9fl oz/1 cup white wine
2 tbsp chopped flat-leaf parsley leaves
2 tbsp chopped mint leaves
6 cherry tomatoes, halved
10 mild-flavoured black olives, pitted
2 large handfuls of rocket (arugula) leaves
salt and freshly ground black pepper
crusty bread, to serve

Fill a large bowl with water and squeeze the juice from 1 of the lemons into the water.

Using a paring knife, trim the stems of the artichokes, leaving 2.5cm/1in remaining. Trim off the tough outers leaves and cut 2.5cm/1in off the top of each artichoke. If they have a choke in the middle, then slice them in half lengthways and scrape out the fuzzy centre with a teaspoon, but if you are using very small baby artichokes then this should not be necessary. Using a vegetable peeler, peel off any remaining hard parts near the base of the stems. As you finish preparing each artichoke, drop it into the acidulated water.

Put the onion, carrot, garlic and olive oil in a large saucepan, season with salt and pepper and cook gently over a medium heat for 5 minutes.

Drain the artichokes and add them to the pan of vegetables with the juice of the second lemon. Pour in the vinegar, honey, wine and half of the parsley and mint. Season well, cover and cook over a medium-high heat for 6 minutes, then turn the heat down to low and cook for a further 10 minutes more until tender.

Remove the lid from the pan, add the tomatoes and olives and cook over a low heat, about 3 minutes.

Place some rocket leaves on each serving plate or a large platter. Scoop the artichokes on top and spoon over the sauce. Scatter over the remaining herbs and serve warm with bread.

GET ORGANIZED
This can be prepared in the morning, but do not add the olives and tomatoes until just before serving.

Cos with roquefort buttermilk dressing

One of my most favourite childhood meals was cooked by my father: grilled steak, a baked potato heaped with soured cream and iceberg (crisphead) lettuce with a Roquefort dressing. This version of the Roquefort dressing is moderately healthier, replacing much of the mayonnaise in the original with buttermilk, but it's equally moreish.

SERVES 4/PREP 15 MINUTES

2 large cos (romaine) hearts
1 small red onion, cut into thin rings
250g/9oz cherry tomatoes, halved
1 large cucumber, peeled and sliced, or
  3 small Lebanese cucumbers, sliced
4 cooked crisp bacon rashers, crumbled

ROQUEFORT BUTTERMILK DRESSING
100ml/3½fl oz/scant ½ cup buttermilk
4 tbsp mayonnaise
60g/2¼oz Roquefort or other blue cheese,
  crumbled
2 tbsp white wine vinegar
1 garlic clove, crushed
3 tbsp chopped chives

Place all the dressing ingredients in a food processor and pulse until the mixture is smooth and creamy, then transfer it to a bowl. Alternatively, mix all the ingredients together in a bowl by hand.

Arrange the salad ingredients in a large serving bowl. Pour the dressing over just before serving.

GET ORGANIZED
The dressing can be made up to 3 days ahead and the salad 4 hours in advance. Add the onion and dressing just before serving.

Roast squash salad with pine nuts and agrodolce dressing

This warm Sicilian sweet and sour dressing is crazy-good on grilled fish or roasted vegetables. Creamy butternut squash is perfect for soaking up all the tart flavours and toasted pine nuts lend some crunch. Serve it with baby kale or rocket leaves.

**SERVES 4/PREP 25 MINUTES/
COOK 20 MINUTES**

2 large butternut squash, peeled, de-seeded
    and cut into chunky pieces
2 tbsp extra virgin olive oil
4 handfuls of baby kale leaves or rocket
    (arugula) leaves
2 tbsp chopped mint leaves
4 tbsp toasted pine nuts
salt and freshly ground black pepper

AGRODOLCE DRESSING
3 tbsp extra virgin olive oil
2 garlic cloves, thinly sliced
3 tbsp red wine vinegar
1½ tbsp clear honey
1 small red onion, thinly sliced
½ tsp dried red chilli flakes

Preheat the oven to 200°C/400°F/Gas Mark 6. Place the squash on a large baking (cookie) sheet. Toss with the olive oil and season with salt and pepper. Roast, shaking the baking sheet occasionally, for about 20 minutes or until golden and tender.

Meanwhile, make the agrodolce dressing. Heat the olive oil in a sauté pan, add the garlic and cook until golden brown. Pour in the vinegar and add the honey, onion and chilli flakes. Bring to the boil, then turn the heat down and simmer for 5 minutes until syrupy.

Transfer the squash to a large dish and drizzle the warm dressing over the top. Place some kale leaves on each plate, spoon the squash on top and sprinkle with the mint and pine nuts.

GET ORGANIZED
The squash can be prepared at least 2 hours ahead. Part-roast, immediately place in the refrigerator and finish off cooking just before serving. The dressing can be made in the morning.

Spinach salad with warm prosciutto and champagne dressing

In the 1970s, spinach salad with hot bacon dressing was all the rage. This modern adaptation is lighter and healthier, but still impressive.

SERVES 4/PREP 20 MINUTES/
COOK 5 MINUTES

200g/7oz baby spinach leaves
350g/12oz small mushrooms, sliced
1 small red onion, cut into thin rings
75g/2½oz/½ cup toasted chopped walnuts
75g/2½oz Parmesan cheese, coarsely grated
  or shaved

PROSCIUTTO AND CHAMPAGNE DRESSING
6 tbsp extra virgin olive oil
12 slices of prosciutto, diced
3 garlic cloves, finely chopped
6 tbsp dry white wine
6 tbsp lemon juice, plus extra if needed
4 tbsp Champagne or white wine vinegar
4 tbsp sugar, plus extra if needed
½ tsp salt

To make the prosciutto and Champagne dressing, heat the olive oil, prosciutto and garlic in a medium saucepan over a medium heat for about 3 minutes. Add the wine, lemon juice, vinegar, sugar and salt, then simmer for about 2 minutes until thickened and syrupy. Remove from the heat and leave to cool slightly, then taste and add more lemon juice or sugar, if necessary.

Place the spinach on a large platter or in a big bowl. Scatter the mushrooms, onion, walnuts and Parmesan on top.

Just before serving, pour the warm dressing over the salad and mix gently.

GET ORGANIZED
The dressing can be made the day before and stored in the refrigerator. The salad can be prepared in the morning, but don't slice or add the onion or pour over the warm dressing until the last minute.

Thai glass noodles with Asian herbs, crispy shallots and chilli-lime dressing

Glistening noodles with aromatic herbs, a sweet and sour dressing and crispy fried shallots – pure bliss. Refreshing for a summer lunch or as a light appetizer for an Asian dinner, this salad also makes a brilliant base for seared tuna slices, prawns (shrimp) or crab.

SERVES 4/PREP 30 MINUTES/ COOK 10 MINUTES

300g/10½oz very thin glass (cellophane or mung bean) noodles
1 large carrot, cut into julienne
1 red onion, finely diced
1 large handful of Thai basil leaves or other basil leaves, roughly torn or left whole
1 large handful of coriander (cilantro) leaves, roughly chopped
1 large handful of mint leaves
2 tbsp crushed salted cashew or peanuts nuts

CHILLI-LIME DRESSING

1 garlic clove, peeled and left whole
1 tsp finely grated fresh root ginger
125ml/4fl oz/½ cup lime juice
1 tbsp soft brown sugar or palm sugar
2 tbsp Thai fish sauce
½ red chilli, de-seeded and chopped
2 tbsp water

CRISPY SHALLOTS

600ml/1 pint/2½ cups groundnut (peanut) or vegetable oil
10 shallots, very thinly sliced
125g/4½ oz/1 cup plain (all-purpose) flour
salt

To make the crispy shallots, heat the oil to 170°C/338°F in a deep, heavy-based saucepan. Toss the shallots in the flour and shake off any excess. Test the temperature of the oil using a thermometer or with a slice of flour-coated shallot; if it sizzles dramatically when added to the pan, the oil is ready. You don't want the oil to be too hot otherwise the shallots will burn instantly.

Using a wire scoop, carefully add the shallots to the hot oil in batches and fry for 2–3 minutes until golden. Drain on kitchen paper (paper towels) and sprinkle with salt, then set aside.

Soak the noodles in a heatproof bowl of boiling water for about 5 minutes or until al dente.

Meanwhile, make the chilli-lime dressing. Using a mortar and pestle, grind the garlic and ginger to a coarse paste. Add the lime juice, sugar, fish sauce, chilli and measured water. Alternatively, you can chop everything by hand, or crush the garlic and ginger and then mix everything in a small bowl. Set aside.

Drain and rinse the noodles under cold water, then dry on kitchen paper (paper towels). Using a pair of scissors, cut the noodles into 15cm/6in lengths so they are easier to mix in. (The Chinese consider it bad luck to do this, but after doing this numerous times, nothing detrimental has happened to me!)

Put the noodles in a large bowl, pour the dressing over and add the carrot, onion, basil, coriander and mint, then toss until combined.

To serve, arrange the noodle salad on a large platter and top with the crispy shallots and cashews.

GET ORGANIZED
The dressing, noodles and vegetables can be prepared the night before and stored in separate airtight containers in the refrigerator. The shallots can be prepared up to 6 hours before using. Do not add the shallots, herbs, dressing and cashews until 2 hours before serving.

Spelt salad with spring vegetables, dill and red wine vinaigrette

My sister, Teresa, was famous for her confetti rice salad. I have modernized her idea by using spelt and spring vegetables. Spelt is similar to barley and far heartier than standard rice because it retains its texture without going soggy, but feel free to substitute your favourite grain. You can now buy good-quality, ready-cooked grains, which makes putting this type of salad together a very simple affair.

SERVES 4/PREP 15 MINUTES/
COOK 5 MINUTES

1 bunch of thin asparagus, trimmed and cut into
   2.5cm/1in pieces
125g/4½oz/1 cup shelled fresh or frozen peas
100g/3½oz fine green beans, trimmed
500g/1lb 2oz cooked spelt or 250g/9oz dry
   spelt, cooked and drained
1 small red onion, finely diced
200g/7oz jar artichokes, drained and cut
   into quarters
20 black olives in oil, drained, pitted and halved
2 tbsp finely chopped dill
2 tbsp finely chopped flat-leaf parsley leaves
2 tbsp finely chopped mint leaves
4 tbsp almonds, roughly chopped

RED WINE VINAIGRETTE
3 tbsp red wine vinegar, plus extra if needed
5 tbsp extra virgin olive oil
1 garlic clove, finely chopped
½ tsp Dijon mustard
1 tsp sugar
½ tsp each salt and freshly ground black pepper,
   plus extra if needed

To make the red wine vinaigrette, put all the vinaigrette ingredients in a screw-top jar and shake well, then set aside.

Blanch the asparagus, peas and beans in a large pan of boiling water until al dente, about 1 minute. Drain and immediately immerse in iced water. Drain again and dry on clean tea towels (dish towels).

Put the cooked spelt in a serving bowl, add the asparagus, peas, beans, onion, artichokes, olives, dill, parsley and mint.

Pour the dressing over the salad and combine well, then taste and add more salt and vinegar, if necessary. Scatter over the almonds just before serving.

GET ORGANIZED
The dressing, blanched vegetables and spelt can be prepared in the morning and stored in the refrigerator until ready to use. The dressed salad will keep for up to 4 hours, but do not add the onion until 1 hour before serving.

Blood orange, fennel, potato and parsley salad with sherry vinaigrette

It wouldn't be the first match to come to mind, but potatoes and oranges pair surprisingly well. Crisp fennel and a sharp sherry vinaigrette make this Spanish-inspired salad a winning combination.

SERVES 4/PREP 15 MINUTES/
COOK 15 MINUTES

4 red-skinned potatoes, left whole
2 fennel bulbs, cored and thinly sliced
1 small red onion, thinly sliced
4 blood or navel oranges, peeled and cut into
  2cm/¾in slices
1 small handful of flat-leaf parsley leaves,
  left whole

SHERRY VINAIGRETTE
2 tbsp sherry vinegar
4 tbsp extra virgin olive oil
½ tsp each salt and freshly ground black pepper,
  plus extra for seasoning

Cook the potatoes in a large pan of salted boiling water until knife tender, about 8-10 minutes. Drain and leave to dry in the warm pan. When cool enough to handle, peel the potatoes and cut them into 2cm/¾in thick slices.

Meanwhile, make the sherry vinaigrette. Put all the ingredients in a screw-top jar and shake well, then set aside.

Arrange the potatoes on a large platter or in a shallow bowl and top with the fennel and onion. Place the oranges on top and sprinkle with the parsley.

Drizzle the dressing over the salad, season to taste with salt and pepper, then serve.

GET ORGANIZED
The salad is best made within 1 hour of serving to keep the ingredients at their freshest.

Spicy peanut noodles

This is loosely based on Sichuan sesame noodles but I use peanut butter in place of the traditional ground sesame seeds. Do try and seek out the chilli bean paste as it really makes this salad. You can find it in most Asian stores or online.

SERVES 4/PREP 15 MINUTES/
COOK 7 MINUTES

450g/1lb dried medium egg noodles or spaghetti
200g/7oz can water chestnuts, drained and
  thinly sliced
8 spring onions (scallions), thinly sliced
salt

SESAME DRESSING
185ml/6fl oz/¾ cup crunchy peanut butter
4 tbsp chilli oil
4 tbsp sesame oil
3 tbsp sugar
4 tbsp soy sauce
4 tbsp red wine vinegar
4 tbsp cold water
2 tbsp hot chilli bean paste

Cook the noodles in a large pan of salted boiling water until al dente, about 7 minutes. Drain and place in a large mixing bowl.

Meanwhile, make the sesame dressing. Using a whisk mix all the ingredients together in a small bowl until combined.

Pour the dressing over the noodles while they are still warm and mix well. When the noodles have cooled slightly, add the water chestnuts and spring onions. Serve while still warm or leave to cool to room temperature.

GET ORGANIZED
The salad can be made the morning of serving, or will keep for 3–4 days in the refrigerator.

Soba noodles with purple sprouting broccoli and sweet soy, ginger and chilli dressing

Soba, chewy Japanese buckwheat noodles, have a distinctive nutty flavour. Traditionally, they're served plain with a soy dipping sauce, but this sweet soy and ginger dressing does them proud. Kecap manis, an Indonesian sauce, is fantastic in Asian dressings as it's sweet and not as salty as regular soy.

SERVES 4/PREP 10 MINUTES/
COOK 6 MINUTES

250g/9oz Japanese soba or somen noodles
400g/14oz purple sprouting or regular broccoli,
   roughly chopped
2 tbsp toasted sesame seeds
salt

SWEET SOY, GINGER AND CHILLI DRESSING
5 tbsp kecap manis (sweet soy sauce)
2 thumb-sized red chillies, de-seeded
   and chopped
2 garlic cloves, finely chopped
1 tbsp finely chopped fresh root ginger
juice of 3 limes
1 tbsp caster (superfine) sugar

Cook the noodles in a pan of boiling water for 5 minutes or until al dente. Soba noodles cook very quickly so check them regularly. Drain the noodles, rinse under cold water and leave in the colander until ready to dress.

Blanch the broccoli in a separate pan of salted boiling water until al dente, about 1 minute. Drain and immediately immerse in iced water. Drain again and dry on kitchen paper (paper towels).

Meanwhile, make the soy, ginger and chilli dressing. Put all the ingredients in a small bowl and mix together. Alternatively, you can blend them in a food processor. Set aside.

Place the noodles and broccoli in a large bowl. Pour the dressing over and mix well. Sprinkle the sesame seeds on top and serve.

GET ORGANIZED
The salad can be fully prepared up to 4 hours before serving. If left for longer, the noodles become too starchy. Hold back dressing the salad and sprinkling with sesame seeds until serving.

Puntarelle salad with anchovy dressing

Puntarelle is a bitter green and white salad leaf related to the chicory and radicchio family. The Romans like to eat it in winter with a tangy lemon and anchovy dressing, and temper the bitterness of the puntarelle by first soaking it in iced water, which crisps up the leaves. If you can't find puntarelle, use chicory or Treviso instead.

SERVES 4/PREP 10 MINUTES, PLUS SOAKING

2 heads of puntarelle, trimmed of tough outer
  leaves, or 4 heads of chicory (Belgian endive)
  or Treviso (red chicory)

ANCHOVY DRESSING
5 Spanish or Italian anchovies in oil, rinsed
1 garlic clove, peeled and left whole
juice of 1 lemon or 1 tbsp white wine vinegar
3 tbsp extra virgin olive oil
freshly ground black pepper

If using puntarelle, split the hollow stalks lengthways into long strips. Soak in iced water for 30 minutes to crisp up, then drain and set aside. Alternatively, cut the chicory or Treviso into diagonal slices.

To make the anchovy dressing, using a mortar and pestle, grind the anchovy fillets and garlic to a paste, then transfer to a small bowl. Whisk in the lemon juice and olive oil and season with pepper.

Arrange the puntarelle leaves in a serving bowl Pour the dressing over the salad just before serving and grind extra pepper over.

GET ORGANIZED
The lettuce can be soaked in the morning, stored in the refrigerator for up to 5 hours, and drained before serving. Make the dressing up to 1 hour before eating, but don't dress the salad until just before serving.

Prawn, pork and pineapple salad with chilli-lime dressing

Pork, prawns and pineapple? Hmmm... stay with me, because this classic Thai salad is a fantastic combination. Sweet pineapple, tender minced pork and succulent large prawns are imbued with a spicy lime dressing and crunchy ginger. Take a walk on the wild side with this exotic dish.

SERVES 4/PREP 20 MINUTES/
COOK 10 MINUTES

Chilli-lime Dressing (see page 65)
1 tbsp vegetable oil
250g/9oz minced (ground) pork
250g/9oz large cooked and peeled prawns
  (shrimp)
1 red (bell) pepper, de-seeded and finely diced
1 small red onion, finely diced
100g/3½oz fresh pineapple, chopped
15g/½oz mint leaves, finely chopped
15g/½oz basil leaves, finely chopped
1 Little Gem (Bibb) lettuce, leaves separated
1 small handful of coriander (cilantro) leaves,
  left whole

Follow the instructions for making the Chill-lime Dressing on page 65, then set aside.

Heat the oil in a sauté pan. Add the pork mince and cook for 10 minutes or until browned, breaking it up with a spoon. Leave to cool slightly, then place in a bowl with the prawns, red pepper, onion, pineapple, mint and basil.

Pour the dressing over and mix gently.

Arrange the lettuce leaves on a large platter and spoon the prawn and pork salad on top. Sprinkle with the coriander and serve immediately.

GET ORGANIZED
All the salad ingredients and the dressing can be prepared earlier in the day and stored in the refrigerator, but assemble just before serving.

Crispy quail, chargrilled aubergines and green beans with pomegranate dressing

There is something slightly comical about grilled quail, with their Lilliputian wings and tiny thighs. Pomegranate molasses, made from boiled, crushed pomegranate seeds, is not only used for vinaigrettes, the sticky-sweet sauce is also perfect for barbecue glazes.

SERVES 4/PREP 25 MINUTES, PLUS MARINATING/COOK 30 MINUTES

4 tbsp pomegranate molasses
1 tsp ground cinnamon
3 garlic cloves, crushed
8 boneless quails or skinless, boneless
   chicken thighs
200g/7oz green beans, trimmed
2 small aubergines (eggplant), cut into
   1cm/½in slices
olive oil, for brushing
15g/½oz flat-leaf parsley leaves, roughly chopped
2 handfuls of baby spinach leaves
1 small red onion, finely diced
seeds of 1 pomegranate
salt and freshly ground black pepper

POMEGRANATE DRESSING
5 tbsp pomegranate molasses
juice of ½ lemon
1 garlic clove, crushed
½ tsp ground cumin
1 tsp sugar
3 tbsp extra virgin olive oil

To make the marinade, combine the pomegranate molasses, cinnamon and garlic in a bowl and season with salt and pepper. Rub the mixture all over the quail or chicken thighs, then leave to marinate, covered, for at least 30 minutes or up to 3 hours in the refrigerator.

Meanwhile, make the pomegranate dressing. Put all the ingredients in a screw-top jar and shake well, then set aside.

Blanch the beans in a pan of boiling water until al dente, about 1 minute. Drain and immediately immerse in iced water. Drain again and set aside.

Brush a small amount of the pomegranate dressing over the aubergine slices and season with salt and pepper. Heat a griddle (grill) pan, brush it with oil and grill the aubergines in batches, about 2 minutes on each side or until they have griddle marks. Remove and set aside.

Grill the quail until crispy and golden and cooked through. If using an outdoor grill, they will take about 8 minutes (4 minutes on each side) or place under a preheated oven grill (broiler) for 5 minutes, turning once. Alternatively, you can roast them in an oven, preheated to 200°C/400°F/Gas Mark 6, for 20 minutes. (If using chicken thighs, they will take slightly longer to cook through; just make sure the juices run clear when they are pierced with a knife and there is no trace of pink.)

Place the parsley leaves on a large platter. Arrange the spinach, beans, aubergines and onion on the parsley and place the quail or chicken on top. Pour the dressing over and sprinkle with the pomegranate seeds.

GET ORGANIZED
The dressing and beans can be prepared in the morning. The quail, or chicken, and aubergines can be cooked 3 hours before eating, but undercook them and finish them in the oven before serving.

Lemon crab, fennel and rocket salad with saffron aioli crostini

Fresh white crabmeat is so magnificent it doesn't need much alteration. I've given it minimal treatment here, just tossed it with lemon, thin slices of raw fennel and wild rocket. Alongside, is a lusty spoonful of saffron aioli and crispy crostini. The aioli recipe will make more than you need for this recipe, but it keeps for 7–10 days refrigerated.

SERVES 4/PREP 20 MINUTES

150g/5½oz fresh white crabmeat
1 red chilli, de-seeded and finely chopped
juice of 1 lemon
100g/3½oz wild rocket (arugula) leaves
1 fennel bulb, cored and very thinly sliced
2 tbsp extra virgin olive oil
8 thin slices of ciabatta or other Italian bread,
    toasted
freshly ground black pepper
lemon wedges, to serve

SAFFRON AIOLI

½ tsp salt, plus extra for seasoning
1 garlic clove, finely chopped
2 egg yolks, at room temperature
1 tbsp Dijon mustard
1 tsp saffron threads, soaked in 1 tbsp hot water
200ml/7fl oz/scant 1 cup vegetable or groundnut
    (peanut) oil
juice of ½ lemon, plus extra if needed

To make the saffron aioli, using a mortar and pestle sprinkle the salt over the garlic and crush it into a paste. Place the egg yolks, mustard, saffron and soaking water, and garlic paste in a food processor or blender and process to combine. With the processor still running, gradually pour in the oil until the mixture thickens and emulsifies. Initially, the oil needs to be drizzled in extremely slowly in order for it to "catch" and thicken up. Once you get past this stage, pouring can speed up. Add the lemon juice and pulse once more. Taste and add additional salt and lemon, if necessary. Alternatively, you can prepare the aioli in a small bowl using a whisk. Cover and refrigerate until ready to use.

Combine the crab, chilli and lemon juice in a bowl. Season well and toss together.

When ready to serve, arrange the rocket and fennel slices on individual serving plates and drizzle over the olive oil. Spread a liberal amount of the aioli on the toasts and place 2 on each plate. Heap the crab mixture on top and serve with lemon wedges for squeezing.

GET ORGANIZED
The aioli and toasts can be made the day before and stored separately in airtight containers in the refrigerator. Everything else should be prepared shortly before serving.

Thai beef salad

The Thais are geniuses when it comes to salad creations and this beef version is a classic. If I had to pick the one recipe I love the most in this book, then this would be it. Substantial with bracing, full-on flavours, it's a glorious creation.

SERVES 4/PREP 20 MINUTES, PLUS MARINATING/COOK 10 MINUTES

800g/1lb 12oz beef fillet (tenderloins) steaks or sirloin or skirt steak
1 tbsp Thai fish sauce
2 tsp crushed black peppercorns
Chilli-lime Dressing (see page 65)
200g/7oz cherry tomatoes, halved
3 Lebanese or other baby cucumbers, cut into slices
2 small shallots, thinly sliced
1 lemongrass stalk, outer layers removed, thinly sliced
1 handful of mint leaves, chopped
1 handful of coriander (cilantro) leaves, chopped
2 tsp dried red chilli flakes

Put the beef in a shallow, non-metallic dish, pour over the fish sauce and add the peppercorns. Turn the beef until coated and leave to marinate for at least 10 minutes or up to 3 hours in the refrigerator.

Heat a large, heavy-based frying pan over a high heat until very hot. Sear the steaks for 2–3 minutes on each side and then remove from the pan and leave to rest, covered, for 10 minutes before slicing thinly. The steaks will be medium-rare if about 4cm/1½in thick. If you want medium or well-done steaks then turn the heat down to low after searing and cook for another 2 minutes on each side. If you have ultra-thick steaks then cook them for another minute on each side.

Meanwhile, follow the instructions for making the Chilli-lime Dressing on page 65 then set aside.

Combine the beef, tomatoes, cucumbers, shallots, lemongrass, mint, coriander and chilli flakes in a bowl. Just before serving, pour the dressing over the salad and combine well.

GET ORGANIZED
All the preparation can be done in the morning, but do not add the dressing and onion until just before serving.

Seared duck with sugared pecans, spinach and raspberry dressing

This "one-dish" duck salad is impressive and simple to make. The depth of flavour is dramatically improved if you marinate the duck breasts for a couple of hours beforehand.

SERVES 4/PREP 20 MINUTES, PLUS MARINATING/COOK 25 MINUTES

2 tbsp raspberry vinegar
2 tbsp soy sauce
4 medium duck breasts
200g/7oz fine green beans, trimmed
100g/3½oz baby spinach leaves
125g/4½oz cherry tomatoes, quartered
1 small red onion, finely diced
freshly ground black pepper

RASPBERRY DRESSING

4 tbsp raspberry vinegar
2 tbsp balsamic vinegar
4 tbsp olive oil
3 tbsp hazelnut or walnut oil
1 tsp Dijon mustard

SUGARED PECANS

50g/1¾oz/½ cup pecans
2 tbsp clear honey
½ tsp salt, plus extra for seasoning
1 tbsp caster (superfine) sugar
2 tsp vegetable oil

Mix together the raspberry vinegar and soy in a shallow, non-metallic dish to make a marinade.

Score a criss-cross pattern on the fat side of the duck breasts with a knife and season well with salt and pepper. Add to the marinade, turning to coat, and leave to marinate in the refrigerator for at least 1 hour and up to 24 hours.

Preheat the oven to 200°C/400°F/Gas Mark 6. Drain the duck breasts, discarding the marinade, and pat dry with kitchen paper (paper towels).

Heat a non-stick sauté pan until very hot. Sear the duck breasts, skin-side down, then turn the heat down to low and cook for about 10 minutes until the fat has rendered. You want the fat to melt slowly, without burning, so that you have a thin, crispy layer of fat.

Transfer the duck to a shallow roasting pan or ovenproof dish and roast in the oven for 10 minutes for medium-rare. Remove from the oven, leave to rest for 10 minutes and then slice thinly.

While the duck is resting, make the sugared pecans. On a baking (cookie) sheet, toss the pecans with the other ingredients until coated then bake for 5 minutes. Remove and leave to crisp up on non-stick baking paper.

Meanwhile, make the raspberry dressing. Put all the ingredients in a screw-top jar, season with salt and pepper and shake well, then set aside.

Blanch the beans in a pan of boiling water until al dente, about 1 minute. Drain and immediately immerse in iced water. Drain again and dry on kitchen paper (paper towels).

Place the spinach on a platter or individual plates. Arrange the beans on top of the spinach with the tomatoes and onion. Place the sliced duck breast on top, drizzle the dressing over and top with the pecans.

GET ORGANIZED
The duck breasts can be marinated and the beans, pecans and dressing can be prepared and stored in the refrigerator the day before serving.

Lamb's lettuce with shredded chicken, sourdough and walnut oil vinaigrette

This salad was inspired by the famous chicken and bread salad from Judy Rodger's Zuni Café in San Francisco. Freshly roasted shredded chicken is tossed with sourdough croûtons and a nut oil and sherry vinaigrette. If you don't feel inclined to roast a whole chicken, buy a ready-roasted one at the supermarket.

SERVES 4/PREP 15 MINUTES/COOK 1 HOUR

1kg/2¼lb whole chicken, preferably organic
200g/7oz sourdough bread, cut into
   2cm/¾in cubes
3 tbsp extra virgin olive oil
Walnut Oil Vinaigrette (see page 49)
4 large handfuls of lamb's lettuce (mâche)
   or other mild salad leaves (greens), such as
   baby spinach
200g/7oz small chestnut (cremini) mushrooms,
   thinly sliced
1 small handful of flat-leaf parsley leaves
50g/1¾oz/½ cup pecans, chopped
1 small red onion, thinly sliced
salt and freshly ground black pepper

Preheat the oven to 200°C/400°F/Gas Mark 6. Place the chicken on a rack set into a roasting pan and season with the salt and pepper. Roast for 60 minutes, until the juices run clear when a skewer is inserted into the thickest part of the meat and it is cooked through, crispy and brown.

Meanwhile, make the sourdough croûtons. Toss the bread cubes in the oil, season with salt and pepper and tip onto a large baking (cookie) sheet. Spread out evenly and toast the croûtons in the oven at the same time as the chicken is roasting for 8–10 minutes until crisp and golden.

Meanwhile, follow the instructions for making the Walnut Oil Vinaigrette on page 49, then set aside. Remove the chicken from the oven and leave it to rest for at least 10 minutes. When cool enough to handle, carve the bird, discarding the skin and bones, then shred the meat with your fingers.

Arrange the lamb's lettuce on a large platter and scatter the chicken over. Add the mushrooms, parsley, pecans, onion and croûtons. Just before serving, pour the dressing over the salad.

GET ORGANIZED
The roast chicken, dressing, croûtons and walnuts can be prepared the day before and stored in airtight containers. Refrigerate the chicken. The salad should be made just before serving.

Tandoori prawns with cucumber and tomato salad

Fat, succulent prawns are marinated in a spiced yogurt, pan-grilled and tossed with refreshing cucumbers, tomatoes and a lime dressing. It's an exotic, healthy salad that will have you daydreaming of the shores of Kerala.

SERVES 4/PREP 20 MINUTES, PLUS MARINATING/COOK 3 MINUTES

400g/14oz large, raw prawns (shrimp), peeled
  and de-veined
200g/7oz Greek or full-fat (whole) yogurt
4 tbsp lemon juice
1 tsp paprika
1 tsp ground cumin
1 tsp garam masala or curry powder
1 tsp finely grated fresh root ginger
1 garlic clove, crushed
4 small Lebanese cucumbers, halved lengthways,
  or 1 large cucumber, halved lengthways
  and de-seeded
1 small red onion, sliced
250g/9oz baby plum or cherry tomatoes, halved
1 tbsp vegetable oil
3 limes, 1 juiced, 2 quartered
1 handful of coriander (cilantro) leaves
salt and freshly ground black pepper
warmed naan or flatbread, to serve

Pat the prawns dry on kitchen paper (paper towels) and set aside.

To make the marinade, combine the yogurt, lemon juice, paprika, cumin, garam masala, ginger, garlic and some salt and pepper in a medium non-metallic bowl.

Remove and reserve 125ml/4fl oz/½ cup of the yogurt marinade and spoon it into a small bowl as an additional salad dressing. Add the prawns to the remaining marinade, coat thoroughly, cover and chill for at least 20 minutes.

Thickly slice the cucumbers or cut into long ribbons with a vegetable peeler. Place them in a bowl with the onion and tomatoes and season to taste with salt and pepper.

Heat a griddle (grill) pan and brush with a little oil to keep the prawns from sticking. Wipe off the excess marinade from the prawns and discard, then grill the prawns until they turn pink and are cooked on both sides, about 2–3 minutes.

Arrange the salad on a platter, squeeze over the lime juice and place the prawns on top. Sprinkle the coriander leaves over the salad and serve with the lime wedges, the reserved yogurt dressing and warm naan or other flatbread.

GET ORGANIZED
The vegetables and marinade can be prepared on the morning of serving and keep refrigerated. Cook the prawns and dress the salad in the lime juice just before serving.

Tuna Sashimi salad with white radish, kumquats and soy, shallot and ginger dressing

I first ate raw tuna at the fashionable London restaurant, Nobu, and I will never forget its memorable taste. If you have quality fish there is no need to sear it. Use only the freshest tuna, shocking red in colour with little or no marbling of fat. Peppery white radish, spicy leaves and sweet kumquats partner alongside and work well with the tart soy dressing.

SERVES 4/PREP 20 MINUTES

500g/1lb 2oz fresh tuna fillet
2 tbsp toasted white or black sesame seeds
30cm/12in white radish (daikon or mooli), cut
  into thin julienne
5 kumquats, thinly sliced and de-seeded
250g/9oz spicy salad leaves (greens) like
  mizuna, baby kale or watercress

SOY, SHALLOT AND GINGER DRESSING
2 tbsp finely chopped shallot
3 tbsp soy sauce
4 tbsp grapefruit, lime or yuzu juice
2 tsp grated fresh root ginger
2 tsp caster (superfine) sugar

To make the soy, shallot and ginger dressing, put all the ingredients in a small bowl and mix together, then set aside.

Cut the tuna lengthways into 2–3 long strips, about 5cm/2in wide, so it looks similar to small beef fillets (tenderloin). Roll the tuna in the sesame seeds and then cut into 1cm/½in slices. Place on individual serving plates or a large platter.

Arrange the white radish to the side of the tuna, then scatter over the kumquats and salad leaves. Spoon the dressing over and serve.

GET ORGANIZED
On the morning of serving, slice the tuna and store in the refrigerator between 2 sheets of non-stick baking paper, loosely covered in cling film (plastic wrap). The radish can be julienned and soaked in cold water and refrigerated. The dressing can be mixed up to 6 hours ahead.

Antipasto salad

Carmine's, an Italian trattoria in New York, serves this house salad family-style on big platters. Artichoke hearts, salami, pickled peppers and crisp lettuce are tossed in a deliciously sweet red wine vinaigrette.

SERVES 4/PREP 15 MINUTES

2 cos (romaine) lettuces, torn into
  2.5cm/1in pieces
2 x 175g/6oz jars marinated artichoke hearts,
  drained
1 handful of pitted black olives, sliced
1 red onion, cut into rings
1 red (bell) pepper, de-seeded and thinly sliced
250g/9oz cherry tomatoes, halved
1 large handful of peppadew or other sweet
  pickled peppers, such as pepperoncini
60g/2¼oz sliced Italian salami, such as
  pepperoni, Napoli picante or Milano

CLASSIC RED WINE VINAIGRETTE
4 tbsp red wine vinegar
7 tbsp extra virgin olive oil
1 garlic clove, finely chopped
½ tsp Dijon mustard
1 tsp sugar
½ tsp each salt and freshly ground black pepper

To make the red wine vinaigrette, put all the ingredients in a screw-top jar and shake well, then set aside.

Place all the salad ingredients in a large bowl.

Just before serving, pour the dressing over the salad and toss well.

GET ORGANIZED
The dressing can be prepared a day ahead and the salad up to 2 hours before serving.

Puy lentils with salami crisps, dill and grainy mustard vinaigrette

When it comes to lentils, Puy are the aristocrats. Unlike other varieties, which tend to disintegrate during cooking, Puy hold their shape magnificently and are coloured a stunning charcoal-green hue. Worth trying, too, are Beluga lentils, which are charcoal black and, like Puy, have a sturdy texture. Lentil salads tend to need other ingredients with a bit of crunch so celery, onions and crisp fried salami come to the rescue, here.

SERVES 4/PREP 20 MINUTES/
COOK 10 MINUTES

250g/9oz/1 cup Puy lentils, rinsed
200g/7oz pepperoni, chorizo or other stick salami, sliced and halved
1 celery heart (the inner part of the celery head), finely chopped
250g/9oz cherry tomatoes, halved
1 small red onion, finely chopped
10 black olives in oil, drained, pitted and sliced
2 tbsp finely chopped dill
3 tbsp finely chopped flat-leaf parsley leaves
freshly ground black pepper

GRAINY MUSTARD VINAIGRETTE
1 garlic clove, finely chopped
4 tbsp extra virgin olive oil
2 tbsp red wine vinegar
1 tbsp balsamic vinegar
1 tbsp grainy mustard
½ tsp salt, plus extra for seasoning

Place the lentils in a saucepan, add cold water to cover and bring to the boil. Boil for 10 minutes or until al dente. Drain the lentils and place in a medium bowl.

Meanwhile, make the grainy mustard vinaigrette. Put all the ingredients in a screw-top jar and shake well, then set aside.

Cook the pepperoni, in a large, dry sauté pan until crisp, then drain on kitchen paper (paper towels). Add to the lentils with the celery, tomatoes, onion, olives, dill and parsley.

Pour the dressing over the lentil salad and mix well. Season with salt and pepper, if necessary.

GET ORGANIZED
The entire salad can be prepared the night before and refrigerated, but don't add the onion and only pour over half of the dressing, then add the remaining dressing and onion just before serving.

Halibut ceviche with mango, red onion and coriander

Refreshing is the first word that comes to mind when I think about ceviche. Slices of halibut are "cooked" in lime juice and paired with juicy mango, red onion and crunchy pieces of corn tortilla. It goes without saying that you should purchase only the highest-quality, freshest-possible fish for this – I find halibut fillets, scallops and tuna work best. Homemade margaritas or caipirinhas are the compulsory cocktails to serve alongside.

SERVES 4/PREP 20 MINUTES, PLUS MARINATING/COOK 10 MINUTES

300g/10½oz halibut fillet, skinned and very
   thinly sliced
250ml/9fl oz/1 cup lime juice
1 tsp salt, plus extra for seasoning
1 tsp caster (superfine) sugar
8 corn tortillas
4 tbsp vegetable oil
1 large ripe mango, peeled, stone removed
   (pitted) and roughly chopped
1 small handful of coriander (cilantro) leaves,
   roughly chopped
1 small red onion, sliced
1 small red chilli, de-seeded and sliced
hot sauce, to serve (I like chipotle Tabasco)

Arrange the halibut slices in a flat non-metallic dish. Pour three-quarters of the lime juice over the fish, sprinkle the salt and sugar over and set aside in the refrigerator for 30–60 minutes or until the fish has turned opaque.

Preheat the oven to 200°C/400°F/Gas Mark 6. Brush both sides of the tortillas with the oil, cut into triangles and arrange on a large baking (cookie) sheet. Bake for 8–9 minutes or until golden, then sprinkle with salt.

Remove the fish from the lime juice, discarding the juice, and place on a serving platter or individual plates. Add the mango, coriander, onion and chilli, then pour the remaining lime juice over and taste for salt, adding more if needed. Serve with the tortilla chips.

GET ORGANIZED
The halibut should not be marinated for longer than 1 hour before serving or it will become rubbery. The lime juice dressing should be poured over just before serving or the mangoes will become slimy. The tortilla chips can be baked the morning of serving.

Frisée and radicchio salad with chopped egg, bacon and red wine vinaigrette

Chopped eggs are SO good with vinaigrette. Frisée, with its slender, yellow-white, curly leaves catches every drop of the dressing, while the crispy bacon and ruby-red radicchio complete this satisfying, yet simple salad.

**SERVES 4/PREP 15 MINUTES/
COOK 7 MINUTES**

3 free-range eggs
1 large head of frisée (curly endive), core and
   dark green outer leaves removed
½ head of radicchio, leaves torn into
   2.5cm/1in pieces
8 thin cooked crispy bacon rashers (strips)
   or pancetta, crumbled

RED WINE VINAIGRETTE
4 tbsp red wine vinegar
7 tbsp extra virgin olive oil
1 garlic clove, finely chopped
½ tsp Dijon mustard
1 tsp sugar
½ tsp each salt and freshly ground black pepper

Bring a small pan of water to the boil. Gently place the eggs in the water and boil for 7 minutes until soft-boiled. Plunge the eggs into cold water to stop any further cooking, then peel and cut in half.

While the eggs are cooking, make the red wine vinaigrette. Put all the ingredients in a screw-top jar and shake well, then set aside.

Arrange the frisée leaves on a large platter and top with the radicchio. Place the chopped soft-boiled egg halves on top followed by the crumbled bacon or pancetta. Pour the dressing over the salad and serve.

GET ORGANIZED
The dressing can be made the day before. The eggs can be cooked up to 2 days in advance and kept unpeeled in the refrigerator. The salad leaves (greens) and bacon can be prepared in the morning.

Fig, mozzarella and basil salad with prosciutto

The difference between a great fig and a bad one is vast, so avoid the green ones and steer towards the juicy purple ones; they come into season twice a year, usually in early summer and late autumn. Remember to serve the mozzarella at room temperature, as chilling alters the cheese's texture. Burrata would also be nice, too, depending on your budget.

SERVES 4/PREP 10 MINUTES

4 buffalo mozzarella balls, drained
8 ripe figs, quartered
2 tbsp toasted hazelnuts, roughly chopped
1 large handful of basil leaves, torn in half
4 tbsp good-quality aged balsamic vinegar
4 tbsp extra virgin olive oil
4 slices of prosciutto
salt and freshly ground black pepper
toasted slices of bread or soft focaccia, to serve

Tear 1 of the balls of mozzarella into 2 pieces and place on a serving plate. Repeat with the remaining mozzarella to make 4 servings.

Arrange the figs around the mozzarella and sprinkle with the hazelnuts and basil, then drizzle the vinegar and oil over. Season with salt and pepper.

Scrunch up the slices of prosciutto and place 1 on top of each serving. Serve with toasted slices of bread or soft focaccia.

GET ORGANIZED
The ingredients can be prepared on the day, but not assembled together until just before serving or the mozzarella will make everything milky.

Index

Acknowledgements

A huge thanks to the team at Pavilion for wanting to reprint one of my favourite cookbooks. Emily, I remember working on the first book with you ten years ago and it was lovely to have the opportunity to republish with you as editor. Victoria, you are a tireless worker at managing the people and details that went into remaking this – thank you so much for your hard work. Laura, you've designed this book beautifully thank you.

Patrick, Liam and Riley you are the rock at the centre of my world and I couldn't do without your discerning taste buds and honest opinions that help shape my cooking.

My assistant, Zoe Harrington, working with you in the last year has been heaven and I couldn't do my job without you. I have yet to see you flustered or lose your cool! Your help on the food styling for this book was amazing.

Jo Harris, thank you for choosing such gorgeous props, they suited the book perfectly. Big thanks to Tony Briscoe for making the long journey to my home to work on this. Your photos look lovely.

First published in the United Kingdom in 2017 by
Pavilion
1 Gower Street
London
WC1E 6HD

Copyright © Pavilion Books Company Ltd, 2017
Text copyright © Jennifer Joyce, 2017

The moral right of the author has been asserted.

ISBN 978-1-91090-487-9

A CIP catalogue record for this book is available from the British Library.

10 9 8 7 6 5 4 3 2 1

Reproduction by
Mission Production Ltd, Hong Kong
Printed and bound by
1010 Printing International Ltd, China

This book can be ordered direct from the publisher at www.pavilionbooks.com